classic

italian

cooking

classic

italian

cooking

hamlyn

This edition first published in the U.K. in 1998 by
Hamlyn, a division of Octopus Publishing Group Limited
2–4 Heron Quays, London E14 4JP

Reprinted 2001

Copyright © 1998, 2001 Octopus Publishing Group Limited

ISBN 0 600 60558 2

Printed in Hong Kong

NOTES

Both metric and imperial measurements have been given in all
recipes. Use one set of measurements only, and not a mixture of
both.

Standard level spoon measurements are used in all recipes.
1 tablespoon = one 15 ml spoon
1 teaspoon = one 5 ml spoon

Meat and poultry should be cooked thoroughly. To test if poultry
is cooked, pierce the flesh through the thickest part with a skewer
or fork – the juices should run clear, never pink or red. Do not re-
freeze poultry that has been frozen previously and thawed.

Do not re-freeze a cooked dish that has been frozen previously.

Eggs should be medium to large unless otherwise stated.
The Department of Health advises that eggs should not be
consumed raw. This book contains dishes made with raw or
lightly cooked eggs. It is prudent for more vulnerable people such
as pregnant and nursing mothers, invalids, the elderly, babies and
young children to avoid uncooked or lightly cooked dishes made
with eggs. Once prepared, these dishes should be kept refrigerated
and used promptly.

Milk should be full fat unless otherwise stated.

Nut and Nut Derivatives
This book includes dishes made with nuts and nut derivatives. It
is advisable for people with known allergic reactions to nuts and
nut derivatives and those who may be potentially vulnerable to
these allergies, such as pregnant and nursing mothers, invalids,
the elderly, babies and children to avoid dishes made with nuts
and nut oils. It is also prudent to check the labels of pre-prepared
ingredients for the possible inclusion of nut derivatives.

Pepper should be freshly ground black pepper unless otherwise
stated.

Fresh herbs should be used, unless otherwise stated. If
unavailable, use dried herbs as an alternative, but halve the
quantities stated.

Measurements for canned food have been given as a standard
metric equivalent.

Ovens should be preheated to the specified temperature
– if using a fan-assisted oven, follow the manufacturer's
instructions for adjusting the time and the temperature.

Vegetarians should look for the 'V' symbol on a cheese to
ensure it is made with vegetarian rennet. There are
vegetarian forms of Parmesan, feta, Cheddar, Cheshire, Red
Leicester, dolcelatte and many goats' cheeses, among others.

Contents

Introduction

It is often said that whereas we all have to eat to live, the Italians live to eat! This is an affectionate and amusing observation underlying an essential truth. It is also an indication of the sheer passion which Italian food inspires in its own land. Internationally, the cuisine is regarded as second to none – although the limited range of dishes that is familiar outside the country belies the rich variety that is available within Italy itself. Visitors to Italy have taken their enthusiasm for its food back to their home countries. That is why Italian restaurants are so enduringly popular. New ones are opening all the time, and cater to all tastes – from the smart pizzerias and bustling cafés favoured by trendy young things to classic *ristorantes* serving traditional dishes.

Cooking Italian Food

You don't have to eat out in restaurants to experience the joys of Italian food. It is surprisingly easy to cook delicious dishes in your own home. This is because Italians have never lost sight of their basic principles in cooking – which means top-quality ingredients simply prepared. The food has generally been known for its rustic simplicity, with pizza and pasta leading the field in popularity. Deep Fried Artichokes, Octopus and Tomato Salad or Swordfish Palermo-style are all very easy to prepare and will make memorable meals, whether you are cooking for your family or entertaining guests. The game dishes provide authentic Italian flavours that will be appreciated by the most sophisticated of palates; and the glorious desserts, whether rich and creamy, or cool and refreshing, will provide a fitting finale to a special evening's dinner.

Eating and relaxing

Modern life is often stressful and fast-moving, so if some of the more relaxed aspects of Italian eating styles can be emulated, so much the better. Family meals in Italy have a light-hearted atmosphere. The cooking found in many households is often far superior to anything served in restaurants. The main meal of the day is an important social occasion, it is the time when all the family can get together and share the day's news and gossip while enjoying scrumptious, home-cooked food. A typical family meal can go on for hours and is really very flexible. It usually consists of a *minestra* (soup, pasta dish or risotto) followed by a main course (*piatto de mezzo*). This might be meat, fish or poultry with one or two vegetables. If the *minestra* course is not included, then an *antipasto* course is served – this could be a mixture of salamis, some stuffed vegetables, or a mixed seafood salad. Often a raw salad

"A typical family meal can go on for hours and is really very flexible."

food store. There are wonderful Italian olive oils, fresh herbs, regional cheeses, tomato purées and passata, shining olives, plain or stuffed, cans of tomatoes, jars of pesto, artichoke hearts, sun-dried tomatoes, capers, tins of anchovies and all kinds of pasta, fresh and dry. Pasta can be a subject of great debate among Italian food lovers. Many are convinced that fresh pasta is far superior to dried. Fortunately, fresh pasta is easy to make at home, with or without a pasta machine. A machine is simple to use and will give you a more uniform result, but it is perfectly possible to make excellent pasta and to cut the dough by hand. Whatever method you use, it is well worth the effort. The salad and vegetable shelves of major supermarkets are excellent sources of fresh herbs (including those growing in pots), wonderful salad leaves and Italian vegetables flown in farm-fresh. Even fashionable vegetables like Cavalo Nero, the deliciously flavoured Italian cabbage are increasingly available at quite reasonable prices. If you plan to do a lot of Italian cooking, then a well-stocked store cupboard is invaluable. You will find it useful to refer to the special features on these and other Italian ingredients that are included throughout the book.

vegetable is served – it is not unusual for a dish of shelled broad beans to appear. These are eaten raw, dipped in salt. The meal often ends with fresh fruit in season, sometimes cheese, and is rounded off with a small cup of good, strong espresso coffee. If the meal is quite special, there may be a more complicated dessert such as a luscious cake or tart or a cooling ice cream. The Italian cook usually shops for these family meals in colourful local food markets and specialist grocery stores. These also provide an endless source of social interest as well as fresh produce in splendid profusion.

Italian ingredients

Nowadays we are very fortunate to have well-stocked supermarkets that offer a dazzling range of Italian ingredients. These enable the average cook to achieve the true flavour of a classic recipe. You can buy many good quality Italian ingredients without going near a specialist

The flowering of Italian cuisine

Italian cooking is incredibly diverse. Technically, there is no 'Italian' food as such; more accurately the cuisine is a collection of classic regional dishes. There are many proud

"The cuisine is a colourful patchwork of local specialities, quirky recipes and customs that would take years to explore fully."

names preceding Italy's great dishes – Venetian, Roman, Sicilian, Bolognese and Neapolitan for example. These traditions of cooking have developed over many centuries and their sources are anchored in several cultures including Roman, Byzantine and Greek. The main outpouring of creativity occurred during the Renaissance however. Every aspect of life was affected during this period – arts, music and food alike. Traders introduced exotic ingredients from other parts of the world, and this new interest in food meant that cookery became an important skill. In Florence, Milan and Rome, the great regional ruling families gave banquets to impress each other with the splendour of their palaces – and their cooks vied to use the new ingredients that arrived in Venice and Genoa on the spice route from the East Indies. Florence was the great centre of Italian cuisine and the Medicis gave wildly extravagant feasts. Caterina de' Medici took the finest Italian chefs with her on her marriage to the French Dauphin in 1553, and she is credited with introducing the art of fine cuisine to the French nation!

Regional variations

Very few visitors to Italy ever get to know the full complexity of its regional differences. The cuisine is a colourful patchwork of local specialities, quirky recipes and customs that would take years to explore fully. It is much easier to appreciate the scope of Italian food by comparing north and south. The north is heavily industrialised and affluent, with fertile soil and a temperate climate while the south is hot, arid and more rural. If you wanted a really quick way of distinguishing the difference between north and south, simply check out the pasta. In the north they eat flat pasta, freshly made with eggs; in the south the tubular variety is commonly used. The northerners cook with butter while the southerners use olive oil.

In general, southern flavours are much stronger because of the use of herbs and aromatics, particularly in sauces.

Rice dishes are characteristic of northern Italian cooking, this is because the Po valley provides abundant supplies of arborio rice, which is perfect for making the region's splendid risottos. One of Lombardy's classic dishes, Risotto Milanese, is justifiably world famous. Other well known products of the north are Parmesan cheese and prosciutto ham, both from Parma. These two are linked by their methods of production. The whey left over from making the cheese is fed to the Parma pigs. The meat from these pigs is then carefully salted and dried, creating a delicately flavoured ham.

Italy is almost completely surrounded by the sea and local fish are a dominant feature of many regional cuisines. Venice is famous for its red and grey mullet, squid, scampi and mussels. In the north excellent freshwater fish – especially eels – are caught in the Lombardy lakes. The southern coastline and the islands of Sardinia and Sicily are famous for their picturesque fishing villages. The boats catch tuna, sardines, swordfish and all kinds of shellfish which are extensively used in local pasta dishes, sauces, stews, soups and salads. Abundant supplies of tomatoes, garlic, herbs and anchovies in the south give their dishes their typical, highly aromatic flavours. Naples is the culinary capital of the south and is believed to be the original home of both pizza and modern day ice cream. Pizzas are baked in open brick ovens and are mostly eaten as casual snacks. Mozzarella, the cheese used for pizza toppings, has been made for hundreds of years in the surrounding countryside of Campania. Its excellent melting qualities make it perfect for using for pizzas and many other cooked dishes.

Wine

Some years Italy is the largest wine producer in the world, and is the second largest exporter to the United Kingdom after France. With wines produced in virtually every region of the country, a huge range of Italian wines is now available in this country and this is increasing all the time. Of these wines, the better quality ones are enlarging their share of the market, giving the lover of Italian wine ample choice whatever his taste and pocket.

There are various categories of classification: the DOC system rules out non-traditional grapes, and ensures the quality of the wine. DOC stands for *Denominazione di Origine Controllata*. Labels bearing the initials IGT denote *Indicazione Geografica Tipica*, which is the equivalent of *Vin de Pays* in France. However, there are very fine, and expensive, wines being produced in Italy outside the restrictions of the DOC system; the first of these were

known as 'Super Tuscans' but producers in other areas have followed suit. These are labelled *Vino da Tavola*, 'table wine' and they are more modern wines, of high quality.

The robust reds from Piemonte include Barola, Barbaresco and Gattinara. All are good with meat and game, wild mushroom risottos, and cheese. Perhaps Italy's most famous wine, Chianti Classico hails from Tuscany. Chianti is a robust red and an excellent wine to drink with roasts, grills and game dishes.

Veneto, the region which stretches from Venice and Verona to the Alps, produces Valpolicella, a lighter red which is an ideal partner for pasta and pizza, as well as roast meats. The white Soave is from the same region, and is one of its most famous wines.

Another famous white wine, from the region south-east of Rome, is Frascati which is extremely popular in this country; it is ideal for summer salads and dining al fresco.

Asti is a light, sweet, sparkling wine it is very drinkable with rich dried-fruit desserts like Christmas pudding.

Fortified such as the well-known Marsala from Sicily, can be sweet or dry. The dry version is drunk as an apéritif and the sweet as a dessert wine, and it is also used to flavour desserts such as zabaglione.

Fresh stock recipes

You will find it very useful to refer to these basic recipes as they are required for many of the recipes throughout the book. A good stock is easy, satisfying and cheap to make, and uses only a few basic ingredients. It is a pity to resort to stock cubes when the flavour of a delicious fresh broth is far preferable. If you are making fish stock you should be able to find the bones you need at your fishmonger.

Once made, the stocks can be frozen when cooled.

Freeze them in small batches in plastic tubs or ice cube trays. When frozen, the cubes can be transferred to clearly labelled plastic bags for ease of storage.

Every cook should be aware that a few basic rules are necessary in the making of a good stock. If you follow them, you will find that your finished dishes will taste much better.

Stock should always be simmered extremely gently, or it will evaporate too quickly and become cloudy. Never add salt to the stock as simmering will reduce it and concentrate the flavour. This will affect the flavour of the finished dish. Any scum that rises to the surface should be removed as it appears, otherwise it will spoil the colour and flavour of the stock.

Beef stock

Place 750 g/1½ lb boneless shin of beef, cubed; 2 onions, chopped; 2–3 carrots, chopped; 2 celery sticks, chopped; 1 bay leaf; 1 bouquet garni (2 parsley sprigs, 2 sprigs thyme and 1 bay leaf) and 4–6 black peppercorns in a large saucepan. Cover with 1.8 litres/3 pints water.

Slowly bring to the boil, and immediately reduce the heat to a slow simmer. Cover with a well-fitting lid and simmer for 4 hours, removing any scum from the surface. Strain the stock through a muslin-lined sieve and leave to cool before refrigerating.

Makes about 1.5 litres/2½ pints
Preparation time: 15 minutes
Cooking time: about 4½ hours

Chicken stock

Chop a cooked chicken carcass into 3 or 4 pieces and place in a large saucepan with the raw giblets and trimmings; 1 onion, roughly chopped; 2 large carrots, roughly chopped; 1 celery stalk, roughly chopped; 1 bay leaf; a few parsley stalks, lightly crushed and 1 thyme sprig. Cover with 1.8 litres/3 pints cold water.

Bring to the boil, removing any scum from the surface. Lower the heat and simmer for 2–2½ hours. Strain the stock through a muslin-lined sieve and leave to cool.

Bring slowly to just below boiling point. Simmer for 20 minutes, removing any scum from the surface. Strain the stock through a muslin-lined sieve and leave to cool completely before refrigerating.

Makes 1.8 litres/3 pints
Preparation time: 10 minutes
Cooking time: 20 minutes

Vegetable stock

This recipe for vegetable stock can be varied to your own taste, and adapted according to what vegetables you have available. For example, you can try adding some fennel for a mild aniseed flavour, or a sliver or orange zest for an added lift. The addition of tomatoes will give the finished stock extra richness of flavour and colour. Remember to avoid using any floury root vegetables as they will case the stock to become cloudy.

Place 500g/1 lb chopped mixed vegetables – for example, equal quantities of carrots, leeks, celery, onion and mushrooms – with 1 garlic clove, 6 peppercorns and 1 bouquet garni (2 parsley sprigs, 2 sprigs thyme and 1 bay leaf) in a pan, and cover with 1.2 litres/2 pints water. Bring to the boil and simmer gently for 30 minutes, skimming off any scum when necessary. Strain, and cool the stock completely before refrigerating.

Makes 1 litre/1¾ pints
Preparation time: 5–10 minutes
Cooking time: about 45 minutes

Makes 1 litre/1¾ pints
Preparation time: 5–10 minutes
Cooking time: about 2½ hours

Fish stock

Please note that when you are purchasing the bones for this stock, you should avoid the bones of oily fish. It is also very important that the stock does not boil.

Place 1½ kg/3 lb fish trimmings and 1 onion, sliced; white part of 1 small leek; 1 celery stalk; 1 bay leaf; 6 parsley stalks; 10 whole peppercorns and 475 ml/16 fl oz dry white wine into a large saucepan. Cover with 1.8 litres /3 pints cold water.

Cook's Tools

Garlic press
Pizza brick
Grater
Rolling pin
Cheese server
Pizza wheel
Mezzaluna
Pasta server

Garlic press

Used to crush garlic cloves to a fine pulp which speeds up cooking and releases all the garlic flavour into food.

Cheese server

A compact slice, usually made of stainless steel, used at the table for cutting thin slices of firm, hard cheese and transferring them to individual plates. It can also be used for slicing shavings from a block of Parmesan.

Mezzaluna

A half moon-shaped blade, with one or two handles, for chopping mushrooms, herbs, etc. using a rocking motion. Mezzalunas some-times come with their own wooden chopping bowl.

Pizza brick

Usually made of terracotta, this is used to bake pizzas and flat breads instead of a baking sheet. It retains the heat well and crisps the bottom of the pizza during baking. Traditional pizzas are always baked on a pizza brick. The brick should have a raised foot to allow an easy grip when removing it from the oven.

Pizza wheel

A multi-purpose implement for cutting out pizzas, pastry and pasta. When choosing a cutter, make sure that the wheel turns freely.

Pasta server

A long-handled spoon, made of stainless steel or plastic, used for transferring pasta from the saucepan to the serving dish. This useful gadget has teeth which grip long strands of pasta firmly but lightly, while the water drains away through the hole in the middle.

Grater

Available as a flat sheet or in a box shape, which is more stable when in use, graters have a selection of different-sized perforations for grating a variety of items

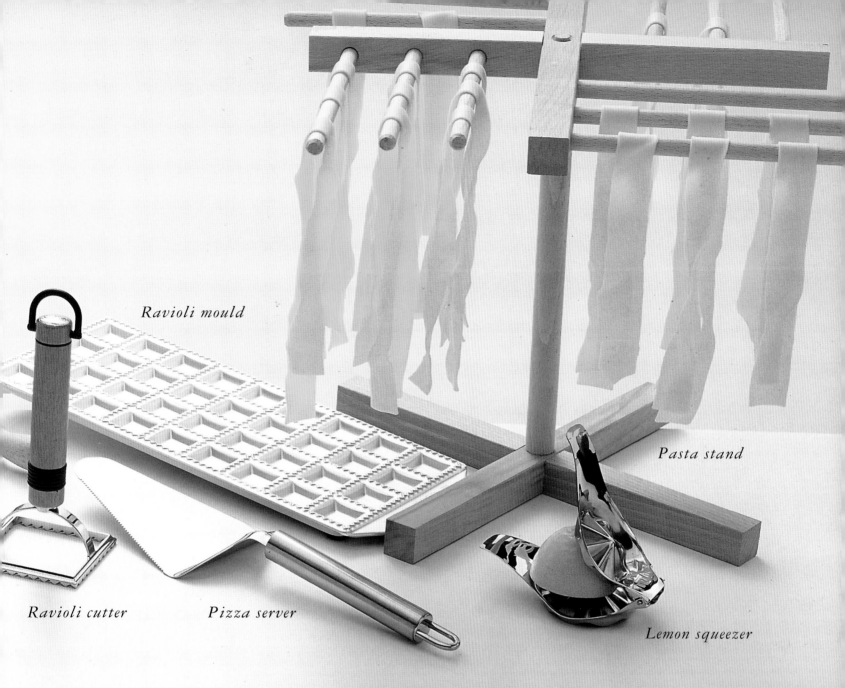

Ravioli mould

Pasta stand

Ravioli cutter

Pizza server

Lemon squeezer

from spices and citrus rind to vegetables and cheese.

Rolling pin

Used for rolling out pasta, bread dough and pastry, rolling pins are usually made of wood or marble. Choose a heavy rolling pin, as this makes rolling easier, and always flour the rolling pin lightly every time you use it to stop it sticking.

Always wipe a rolling pin before putting it away.

Ravioli cutter

A fluted edged metal cutter with a wooden handle, used for stamping out individual raviolis or other flat pasta shapes. It is made in variety of shapes and sizes.

Ravioli mould

A metal tray with a series of

indentations for cutting out ravioli shapes in large numbers. A small rolling pin is sometimes provided with a ravioli mould.

Pizza server

A wide-bladed slice, usually made of stainless steel, used for transferring pizzas from the serving dish to individual plates. It can also double as a pie server.

Pasta stand

This wooden stand for drying homemade pasta is a must for serious home pasta-makers and sweeps away all the awkward Heath Robinson methods of precariously drying pasta over the backs of chairs and broom handles. The stand comes apart and can be packed away in its box for ease of storage.

Lemon squeezer

These are available in a wide range of shapes and sizes. The lemon squeezer pictured above is designed for use at the table, pressing the juice from the lemon slice or half lemon between the two curved surfaces and must be used over the food. The traditional lemon squeezer, always has a saucer to catch the juice.

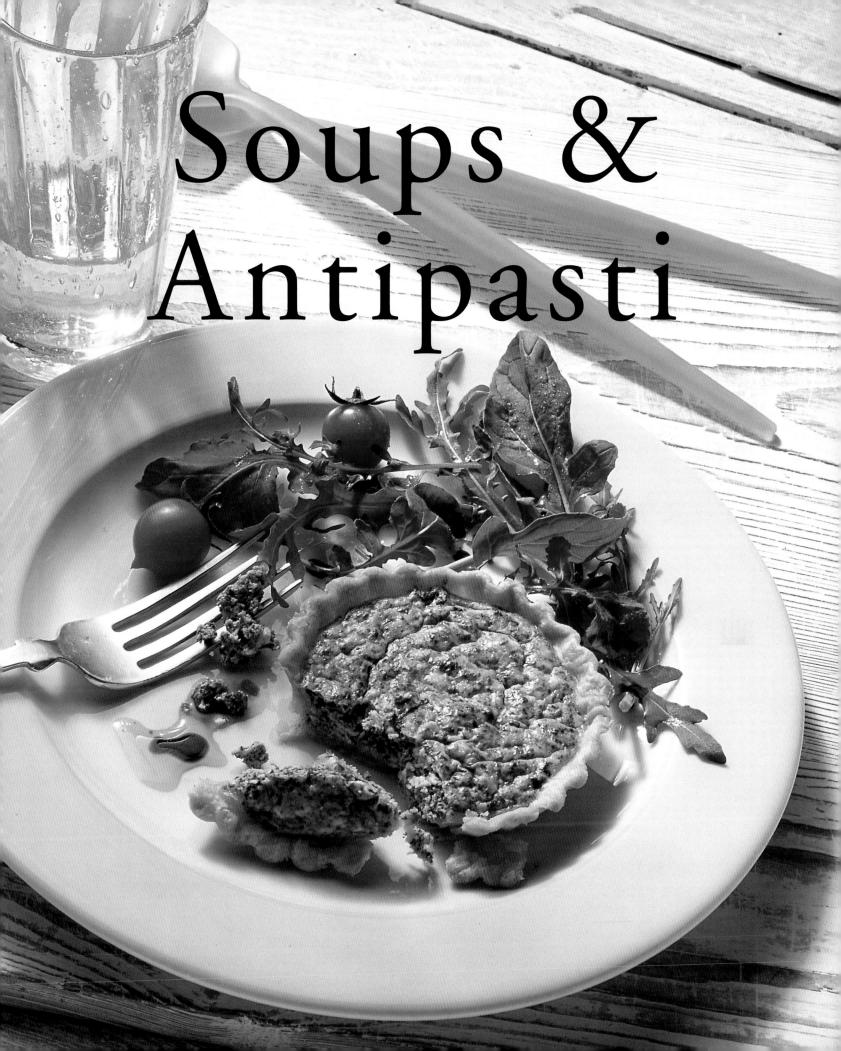

Soups & Antipasti

Minestrone Verde

with red pesto

50 g/2 oz dried haricot or cannellini beans, soaked
overnight

3 tablespoons olive oil

2 garlic cloves, crushed

1 celery stick, finely chopped

2 leeks, cut into rounds

3 tomatoes, skinned and chopped

3 tablespoons chopped flat leaf parsley

1 tablespoon chopped basil

1 tablespoon chopped chives

125 g/4 oz French beans, cut into
2.5 cm/1 inch pieces

125 g/4 oz asparagus, cut into 2.5 cm/1 inch pieces

150 g/5 oz shelled broad beans, defrosted if frozen,
skinned

125 g/4 oz shelled peas, fresh or frozen

1 litre/1¾ pints Vegetable or Chicken Stock (see
pages 10 and 11) or boiling water

75 g/3 oz long-grain rice

175 g/6 oz fresh spinach

salt and pepper

50 g/2 oz Parmesan cheese, finely grated, to serve

Red pesto

2 garlic cloves, chopped

25 g/1 oz basil leaves

3 tablespoons pine nuts

8 sun-dried tomatoes in oil, drained

125 ml/4 fl oz extra virgin olive oil

25 g/1 oz grated Parmesan cheese

drain and rinse the dried beans, place in a saucepan and cover with cold water. Bring to the boil, reduce the heat and simmer for 45 minutes–1 hour or until tender. Remove from the heat and set aside in their cooking liquid.

to make the pesto, place the garlic, basil, pine nuts and sun-dried tomatoes in a food processor or blender and process until finely chopped. With the motor running, gradually add the extra virgin olive oil in a thin stream until blended. Scrape into a bowl, stir in the Parmesan and season to taste with salt and pepper. Set aside.

heat the oil in a large saucepan, add the garlic, celery and leeks and cook gently for 5–10 minutes until softened. Add the tomatoes with half of the herbs, season with salt and pepper and cook for about 12–15 minutes until the tomatoes are soft.

add the French beans, asparagus and fresh broad beans and peas, if using. Cook for 1–2 minutes, then add the stock or water. Bring to the boil and boil rapidly for 10 minutes. Add the rice, the cooked haricot or cannellini beans and their cooking liquid and the spinach (and the frozen broad beans and peas, if using) and cook for 10 minutes. Adjust the seasoning to taste and stir in the remaining herbs. Serve each bowl of soup with a spoonful of pesto, and sprinkle with the Parmesan.

Serves 4–6
Preparation time: *30 minutes, plus soaking*
Cooking time: *about 2 hours*

Pumpkin Soup

The bright orange pumpkin is popular in Italian cooking and is used as both a fruit and a vegetable. Pumpkins have a delicate flavour and are low in calories.

50 g/2 oz butter or margarine
750 g/1½ lb pumpkin, peeled, deseeded and cut into large pieces
150 ml/¼ pint warm water
¼ teaspoon grated nutmeg
pinch of dried thyme
1.5 litres/2½ pints milk
50 g/2 oz long-grain rice
salt and white pepper

Croûtons
3–4 slices white or brown bread, crusts removed
3–4 tablespoons olive oil

melt the butter or margarine in a large saucepan. Add the pumpkin. Stir well and cook over a low to moderate heat for 10 minutes. Add the warm water, nutmeg and thyme with salt and pepper to taste. Cover and cook quickly over a high heat until the pumpkin is soft.

purée the pumpkin mixture in a food processor or blender (in batches if necessary) with a little milk until smooth. Alternatively, rub through a sieve. Scrape the purée into a clean saucepan.

add the remaining milk and the rice to the pumpkin purée in the pan. Stir well and cook, covered, for 30 minutes or until the rice is tender. Stir from time to time.

make the croûtons by cutting the bread into 1 cm/½ inch cubes. Heat the oil in a frying pan, add the bread and fry, turning frequently, until golden brown. Using a slotted spoon transfer the croûtons to kitchen paper to drain. Serve the pumpkin soup in warmed bowls garnished with the croûtons.

Serves 6
Preparation time: *about 10 minutes*
Cooking time: *40–45 minutes*

La Ribollita

This is one of Tuscany's most famous soups. Its Italian name 'ribollita' means reboiled, and refers to the fact that in the old days the soup was reheated and served day after day.

250 g/8 oz dried cannellini beans, soaked overnight
6 tablespoons olive oil
2 onions, roughly chopped
2 carrots, thickly sliced into rings
2 celery sticks, roughly chopped
2 potatoes, roughly chopped
4 tablespoons passata (Italian sieved tomatoes)
250 g/8 oz Savoy cabbage, finely shredded
1.2 litres/2 pints water
pinch of dried rosemary
pinch of dried thyme
125 g/4 oz stale white bread, crusts removed
salt and pepper

drain the beans and rinse under cold running water. Place them in a large saucepan, cover with fresh cold water and bring to the boil. Boil rapidly for 10 minutes, then lower the heat and half cover with a lid. Simmer for 1½ hours or until the beans are tender, skimming off the scum and topping up the water level as necessary.

transfer about half of the beans and their liquid to a food processor or blender and work until smooth. Alternatively, rub through a sieve.

heat 4 tablespoons of the oil in a saucepan, add the vegetables and cook gently, stirring frequently, for 10 minutes until softened.

add the passata and puréed beans and stir well to mix, then add the cabbage, water, rosemary, thyme and salt and pepper to taste. Bring to the boil, then cover and simmer gently for 1 hour.

tear the bread into the soup and add the whole beans and their liquid. Stir well to mix, then simmer for 10 minutes longer. Check the seasoning. Serve hot, drizzled with the remaining oil.

Serves 6
Preparation time: *20 minutes, plus soaking*
Cooking time: *2½ hours*

Spinach and Broccoli Soup

2 tablespoons olive oil

50 g/2 oz butter

I onion, diced

I garlic clove, chopped

2 potatoes, chopped

250 g/8 oz broccoli, chopped

300 g/10 oz spinach, washed and chopped

900 ml/1½ pints Chicken or Vegetable Stock (see pages 10 and 11)

125 g/4 oz Gorgonzola cheese, crumbled into small pieces

juice of ½ lemon

½ teaspoon grated nutmeg

salt and pepper

75 g/3 oz toasted pine nuts, to garnish

warm crusty bread, to serve

heat the oil and butter in a saucepan, add the onion and garlic and sauté for 3 minutes.

add the chopped potatoes, broccoli, spinach and stock, bring to the boil and simmer for 15 minutes.

add the Gorgonzola to the soup with the lemon juice, nutmeg and salt and pepper to taste. This soup can be liquidized or left with chunky pieces according to taste. Garnish with the toasted pine nuts and serve with warm crusty bread.

Serves 4
Preparation time: *10 minutes*
Cooking time: *20 minutes*

Tuscan Bean Soup

In the past the country people made a version of this soup by putting the beans in a large round-bottomed chianti bottle, topping it up with oil and water, garlic and herbs, and leaving it overnight in the embers of the fire.

2 tablespoons olive oil

4 shallots, chopped

2 garlic cloves, chopped

150 g/5 oz piece of unsmoked bacon, diced

1 carrot, diced

2 celery sticks, diced

½ red pepper, cored, deseeded and diced

425 g/14 oz can borlotti beans, drained and rinsed

1 litre/1¾ pints Chicken Stock (see page 10)

1 bay leaf

1 teaspoon chopped oregano

1 teaspoon chopped marjoram

handful of flat leaf parsley, chopped

salt and black pepper

extra virgin olive oil, to finish

heat the oil in a saucepan, add the shallots, garlic, bacon, carrot, celery and red pepper and cook, stirring occasionally, for 5 minutes.

add the beans, stock, bay leaf, oregano and marjoram, bring to the boil and simmer for 15 minutes. Skim off any scum that may come from the beans.

taste and season well. Finally, just before serving, remove the bay leaf and add the chopped parsley.

ladle the soup into warmed bowls and drizzle each one with a little extra virgin olive oil.

Serves 4
Preparation time: *10 minutes*
Cooking time: *25 minutes*

Zuppa di Zucchini *al Basilico*

4 tablespoons olive oil
25 g/1 oz butter, softened
1 large onion, finely chopped
750 g/1½ lb courgettes, sliced
2 potatoes, diced
1.5 litres/2½ pints Chicken Stock (see page 10)
12 basil leaves, finely chopped
1 garlic clove, finely chopped
2 eggs
25 g/1 oz Parmesan cheese, grated
salt and pepper

To serve

6 slices crusty bread
grated Parmesan cheese (optional)

heat the oil and half of the butter in a deep heavy-based saucepan and fry the onion over a low heat until soft but not coloured.

add the courgettes, mix well and fry over a low heat for about 10 minutes.

add the potatoes to the pan and stir over a moderate heat for 3–4 minutes then add the chicken stock. Bring slowly to the boil, cover the pan and simmer over a moderate heat for 40 minutes. Purée the soup in a food processor or blender (in batches if necessary) until smooth. Alternatively, rub the soup through a sieve.

put the basil in a large bowl with the garlic, eggs, the remaining butter and the Parmesan, then beat with a wooden spoon or whisk. Trickle the soup into the beaten egg mixture and season with salt and pepper. Return the soup to the pan and reheat gently over a low heat.

place a slice of crusty bread at the bottom of each warmed soup bowl and pour over the hot soup. Serve immediately, sprinkled with Parmesan if liked.

Serves 6
Preparation time: *15 minutes*
Cooking time: *1 hour*

Country Bread
with olive oil and garlic

This very simple antipasto is traditionally made with sourdough bread at olive harvest time in late autumn. Bruschetta is its best-known name outside Tuscany, but locally it is also called fettunta.

4 large slices country bread
2 large garlic cloves, halved
8 tablespoons extra virgin olive oil
coarse sea or rock salt

toast the bread on both sides under a preheated grill until light golden. While the bread is warm, rub one side with the cut sides of the garlic.

place the bread on a plate and drizzle 2 tablespoons of the olive oil over each slice. Sprinkle with salt to taste and serve immediately.

Serves 2–4
Preparation time: *5 minutes*
Cooking time: *4 minutes*

clipboard: To match the flavour of the first pressing of Tuscan olives, use the best extra virgin olive oil you can afford; the fruity, green olive oil from Lucca is one of the best.

Tuscans like to toast their bread over an open fire – the word bruschetta comes from *bruscare*, meaning 'roast over coals'. You can do this too, or you could chargrill it on a cast-iron grill pan on top of the stove. Look for a close-textured bread such as *pugliese* – it is better for bruschetta than the open-textured ciabatta.

Crostini

2 red peppers
8 slices ciabatta bread
2 garlic cloves, peeled
small handful of flat leaf parsley, chopped
5 tablespoons olive oil
75 g/3 oz black olives, pitted
125 g/4 oz goats' cheese, crumbled
salt and pepper

grill the red peppers on a foil-lined grill pan under a preheated grill for 15–20 minutes, turning frequently until charred on all sides. Transfer to a plastic bag and leave until cool enough to handle.

toast the bread on both sides under a preheated grill until golden brown.

rub the garlic over the bread on one side; the bread acts as a grater and the garlic is evenly spread over the bread. Sprinkle with parsley and salt and drizzle with olive oil.

peel and deseed the peppers and cut the flesh into strips.

mix together the red peppers, olives and crumbled goats' cheese and season with pepper.

spread the mixture evenly over the toasted bruschetta and place under a preheated low grill for 2 minutes until the cheese is just melted. Serve immediately.

Serves 4
Preparation time: *10 minutes*
Cooking time: *20–25 minutes*

clipboard: Sliced tomatoes, sprinkled with oregano and pepper, make another very good crostini topping.

Mixed Antipasti

250 g/8 oz asparagus, cooked and cooled
125 g/4 oz or 4 slices smoked salmon
200 g/7 oz can tuna, drained
250 g/8 oz can artichoke hearts, drained
125 g/4 oz can sardines
125 g/4 oz mozzarella cheese, sliced
2 hard-boiled eggs, shelled and quartered
125–175 g/4–6 oz cooked peeled prawns
125 g/4 oz black olives
olive oil
salt and pepper
lemon wedges, to serve

wrap each slice of smoked salmon loosely around the middle of 3–4 spears of asparagus.

arrange all the other ingredients decoratively on a large platter. Season with salt and pepper and drizzle a little oil over the fish. Cover closely and refrigerate until required.

serve with lemon wedges.

Serves 4
Preparation time: *20 minutes, plus chilling*

clipboard: The original Italian name for this dish is *Antipasto Volente*. *Volente* is roughly translated as 'how it comes', meaning you can use any selection of cold food that you like. Fish and shellfish, slices of cheese, Parma ham or salami and fruits such as slices of melon and sliced fresh figs are typically Italian and combine very well.

Grilled Radicchio

with pears and Gorgonzola

This is an unusual and delicious appetizer and has a lovely combination of flavours. It is also excellent cooked over the barbecue in summer.

4 ripe pears
juice and finely grated rind of 2 oranges
4 tablespoons clear honey
4 small heads radicchio, cut into quarters
1 tablespoon walnut oil
125 g/4 oz Gorgonzola cheese, crumbled
pepper

cut each pear into quarters lengthways and remove the cores. Place the pears in a single layer on a large double-thickness sheet of kitchen foil, turning up the edges slightly. Mix the orange juice, rind and honey in a bowl. Pour over the pears. Bring up the edges of the kitchen foil and press together to seal. Place the parcel in a heavy-based frying pan and cook over a moderate heat for about 15–20 minutes, or until the pears are tender.

start to cook the radicchio about 6 minutes before the pears are ready. Brush the radicchio quarters with the walnut oil and cook under a preheated grill for 2–3 minutes on each side.

divide the pears and their cooking juices between 4 plates. Add 4 radicchio quarters to each portion, then sprinkle with the crumbled Gorgonzola and a little pepper. Serve immediately.

Serves 4
Preparation time: *5 minutes*
Cooking time: *15–20 minutes*

Deep-fried Globe Artichokes

You do not have to use baby artichokes for this dish. If you want to use larger artichokes pre-cook them before deep-frying. Baby artichokes are available from good supermarkets or specialist greengrocers.

12 baby globe artichokes
1 lemon, halved
4 tablespoons flour
vegetable oil, for deep-frying
salt and pepper
lemon wedges, to garnish

trim the artichokes and cut each one lengthways in half or quarters depending on their size. Rub all over the cut surfaces with the halved lemon.

heat 5 cm/2 inches vegetable oil in a deep frying pan until it reaches 180–190°C (350–375°F), or until a cube of bread browns in 30 seconds.

season the flour with salt and pepper, and use to coat the artichokes, then deep-fry them in batches for 1–2 minutes until crisp and golden. Drain on kitchen paper. Serve sprinkled with salt and garnished with lemon wedges.

Serves 4
Preparation time: *20 minutes*
Cooking time: *1–2 minutes each batch*

Mixed Fried Seafood

Fritto misto mare – *mixed fried fish – of various sorts is found in trattorias all around the Italian coast.*

125–175 g/4–6 oz prepared squid, sliced
125–175 g/4–6 oz whitebait
125–175 g/4–6 oz large prawns
125–175 g/4–6 oz plaice fillets, skinned and cut into 1 cm/½ inch strips
125 g/4 oz plain flour
vegetable oil, for deep-frying
salt and pepper
1–2 lemons, sliced or quartered, to garnish

wash all the seafood and dry thoroughly on kitchen paper. Season the flour well with salt and pepper.

heat the oil in a deep pan to 180–190°C (350–375°F), or until a cube of bread browns in 30 seconds. Toss the fish, a batch at a time, in the seasoned flour then fry until golden brown. Drain well on kitchen paper, place on a warmed serving dish and keep hot. Just before serving, sprinkle the fish lightly with salt and garnish with the lemon.

Serves 4
Preparation time: *30–40 minutes*
Cooking time: *15–20 minutes*

clipboard: Any selection of small fish or pieces of fish can be used for this dish, such as queen scallops, pieces of skate or monkfish, cooked shelled mussels, small peeled prawns, sprats or smelts. The quantities given are a guide only; you may prefer more or less of one type of fish.

Grilled Mussels

20 large fresh mussels
25 g/1 oz basil leaves
1 garlic clove, crushed
1 small red chilli, deseeded and diced
½ teaspoon grated lemon rind
1 tablespoon pine nuts
1 tablespoon grated Parmesan cheese
2 tablespoons fresh breadcrumbs
3–4 tablespoons extra virgin olive oil
salt and pepper

scrub the mussels well to remove any barnacles, and then remove the beards. Rinse thoroughly. Put the mussels into a large saucepan and steam them with only the water on their shells for 4 minutes until they have just opened. Discard any that do not open. Immediately plunge the mussels into cold water, and drain.

lift out the mussels and carefully discard one half of each shell. Arrange the cooked mussels in their half shells in a single layer on a large dish or 4 individual gratin dishes.

combine the basil, garlic, chilli, lemon rind, pine nuts, Parmesan and half of the breadcrumbs in a food processor or blender. Process briefly to form a smooth paste and season to taste with salt and pepper. Alternatively, pound to a paste using a pestle and mortar.

transfer the basil paste to a bowl and stir in the oil. Spoon a little of the paste over each mussel and finally top each one with a few more breadcrumbs. Cook under a preheated grill for 2–3 minutes until bubbling and golden. Serve at once.

Serves 4
Preparation time: *15 minutes*
Cooking time: *6–7 minutes*

Marinated Fried Skate

750 g–1 kg/1½–2 lb skate wings, cut into pieces
125 ml/4 fl oz white wine vinegar
125 ml/4 fl oz olive oil
1 onion, sliced
1 bay leaf
1 thyme sprig
3 eggs, beaten
4–6 tablespoons plain flour
handful of flat leaf parsley sprigs
vegetable oil, for deep-frying
salt and pepper
1–2 lemons, sliced or quartered, to garnish

place the skate in a large pan, cover with water, and add 1 tablespoon salt. Bring to the boil and simmer gently for 10 minutes. Cool, then remove the skate from the water and drain well. Remove any thick pieces of bone and place the fish in a shallow dish.

meanwhile, make the marinade. Mix together the vinegar and olive oil with 1 teaspoon salt and ¼ teaspoon pepper. Place the onion, bay leaf and thyme on the fish and pour the marinade over. Cover and refrigerate for 2–3 hours, turning the fish occasionally. Drain and dry the fish well.

heat the oil to 180–190°C (350–375°F) or until a cube of bread browns in 30 seconds. Dip each piece of fish into the beaten eggs and then into the flour and deep fry until golden brown. Drain on kitchen paper and place on a hot serving dish. Fry the parsley in the hot oil. Arrange on the dish with the fish and garnish with the lemon.

Serves 4
Preparation time: *20–30 minutes,*
plus cooling and marinating
Cooking time: *25–30 minutes*

clipboard: In some parts of Italy, this dish is eaten cold. Instead of marinating before frying, simmer and deep-fry the fish as in the recipe then make the marinade with an extra 150 ml/¼ pint white wine vinegar and without the onion. Bring the marinade to the boil, pour it over the fish, and cover and refrigerate overnight or until chilled.

Storecupboard

Capers

Green olives

Borlotti beans

Caperberries

Black olives

Anchovies

Pesto

Tuna

Polenta

Pine nuts

Green olives
These are unripened olives, Buy them canned, bottled, in plastic packets or by the scoop from the barrel. Green olives are also sold stuffed with anchovies, almonds or pimientos.

Polenta
Once a peasant food, and slow and tedious to cook, this vivid yellow Italian cornmeal is now available in 'instant' form which cooks in 6–8 minutes. It has also made the leap to the tables of smart restaurants.

Capers
The small gray-green flower buds of a Mediterranean plant, capers are sold salted or in vinegar. Frequently used in Italian cooking, especially in sharp sauces.

Borlotti beans
These red and white speckled beans are sold dried and canned.

Caperberries
Large caper buds are sometimes sold labelled as caperberries.

Anchovies
Packed in oil or brine, anchovy fillets are an essential ingredient of many Italian dishes.

Pine nuts
Also called pine kernels, these soft little nuts are very rich and have a waxy texture. An indispensible ingredient of pesto.

Pesto
A sauce made from basil, garlic, olive oil, Parmesan cheese and pine nuts, pesto comes from Liguria. It is delicious with pasta.

Black olives
Sold in the same ways as green olives, in their unripened form, black olives have a more gentle flavour.

Tuna
Tuna responds well to the canning process. Look for

Bottled tomatoes

Balsamic vinegar

Mineral water

Olive oil

Olive oil

Artichoke hearts

Red peppers

Canned tomatoes

Risotto rice

Sun-dried tomatoes

Cannellini beans

cans containing chunks, rather than flakes, of skipjack tuna packed in oil or brine.

Bottled tomatoes and cannned tomatoes

It is impossible to imagine Italian cooking without the tomato. Canned and bottled tomatoes are available whole, chopped and sieved (passata), with or without a flavouring of herbs.

Risotto rice

A medium-grain rice which cooks to a soft creamy texture. The best types are arborio and carnaroli rice.

Balsamic vinegar

The undisputed aristocrat of vinegars, *aceto balsamico,* from Modena in northern Italy, has an incomparable sweetness and depth not found in other vinegars.

Mineral water

Still and fizzy mineral water are an essential ingredient for every kitchen and home bar.

Olive oil

The best-known Italian olive oils come from Apulia, Tuscany and Umbria. Look for extra virgin olive oil which is made from olives which are not subjected to any chemical treatment.

Sun-dried tomatoes

These may be sold dried, in which case they must be reconstituted, or packed in oil. They have an intense tomato flavour.

Cannellini beans

These are white kidney beans and are available both dried and canned. Like borlotti beans, they are good in salads and soups.

Red peppers

Sometimes labelled as pimientos, these peeled and deseeded red peppers are usually sold bottled but occasionally in cans.

Artichoke hearts

These can be found in canned and bottled form. They make an excellent starter when combined with a good homemade dressing.

Swordfish Palermo-style

This recipe comes from Sicily, where the swordfish are reputed to be the finest in the world.

4 swordfish steaks, about 250 g/8 oz each
flour, for dusting
125 ml/4 fl oz olive oil
2 garlic cloves
4 anchovy fillets, finely chopped
1 onion, finely chopped
4 tomatoes, skinned, deseeded and chopped
pinch of dried rosemary, crumbled
12 green olives, pitted and sliced
1 tablespoon capers
salt and pepper
2 tablespoons chopped rosemary, to garnish

wash the swordfish steaks and pat them dry with kitchen paper. Sprinkle them with salt and dust lightly with flour on both sides.

heat the olive oil and fry the garlic cloves over a low heat until golden. Discard the garlic and brown the swordfish steaks in the same oil, turning them once. Remove and keep warm.

add the anchovies and onion to the oil and fry until the onions are golden and the anchovies are reduced to a purée. Add the tomatoes and rosemary and simmer gently for 30 minutes, until reduced and thickened.

add the olives and capers and season to taste with salt and pepper. Return the swordfish steaks to the sauce and then heat through very gently. Serve garnished with the chopped rosemary.

Serves 4
Preparation time: *15 minutes*
Cooking time: *45 minutes*

Trota in Cartoccio

Trout is a favourite freshwater fish all over Italy.

2 tablespoons olive oil
2 garlic cloves, crushed
1 onion, chopped
1 celery stick, chopped
4 rosemary sprigs
2 tablespoons dry white wine
2 x 375 g/12 oz trout, cleaned
salt and pepper
rosemary sprigs, to garnish

heat the olive oil in a frying pan and add the garlic, onion and celery. Fry gently for about 5 minutes until soft and golden. Add salt and pepper, 2 of the rosemary sprigs and the white wine. Cook gently for 5 minutes.

cut out 2 double sheets of greaseproof paper large enough to enclose the trout. Brush the paper lightly with a little oil. Divide the sautéed onion mixture equally between the 2 pieces of paper.

wash the trout and dry well with kitchen paper. Sprinkle inside and out with salt and pepper. Place one trout on top of the onion mixture on each piece of paper and top with a sprig of rosemary.

fold the paper over the trout and wrap loosely, securing the sides with a double fold and double folding the ends. Place the parcels on a baking sheet and cook in a preheated oven at 180°C/350°F/Gas Mark 4 for 20 minutes until the fish are cooked and tender. Remove the trout from the paper and serve garnished with sprigs of rosemary.

Serves 2
Preparation time: *10–15 minutes*
Cooking time: *30 minutes*
Oven temperature:
  180°C/350°F/Gas Mark 4

Tonno Fresco alla Marinara

Fresh tuna in a rich sauce with tomatoes, anchovies, olives, parsley and basil makes a splendid summer meal.

4 fresh tuna steaks, about 150 g/5 oz each

flour, for dusting

3 tablespoons olive oil

I onion, chopped

3 garlic cloves, crushed

750 g/1½ lb tomatoes, skinned and chopped

2 tablespoons chopped parsley

few basil leaves, chopped

I bay leaf

4 anchovy fillets, mashed

8 black olives

salt and pepper

wash the tuna steaks and pat dry with kitchen paper. Season with salt and plenty of pepper then dust the steaks lightly with flour.

heat half of the olive oil in a large shallow frying pan and sauté the tuna steaks until golden on one side. Turn them and cook the other side until golden. Carefully remove them from the pan and keep them warm.

add the remaining oil to the pan and sauté the onion and garlic for about 5 minutes, until golden and soft. Add the tomatoes, parsley, basil, bay leaf and anchovies and stir well. Bring to the boil and continue boiling until the mixture reduces and thickens slightly.

return the tuna steaks to the pan, season to taste and simmer gently for 15 minutes, turning once. Turn off the heat, add the olives and leave to stand for 5 minutes. Discard the bay leaf and transfer the tuna steaks in their sauce to a warmed serving dish.

Serves 4
Preparation time: *15 minutes*
Cooking time: *30 minutes*

Sole Marsala
with Parmesan cheese

The cheese and wine in this recipe make a rich, luxurious sauce for the fish. Ideally, Dover sole should be used, as it is the finest quality. Lemon sole makes a perfectly good substitute, but it will have a different flavour.

flour, for dusting
4 Dover or lemon sole, skinned
75 g/3 oz butter
25 g/1 oz Parmesan cheese, grated
50 ml/2 fl oz Fish Stock (see page 11)
3 tablespoons Marsala or dry white wine
salt and pepper
Parmesan cheese, grated, to serve

To garnish
sprigs of flat leaf parsley
lemon wedges

place some flour in a shallow bowl and season with salt and pepper. Dip the sole into the seasoned flour to dust them lightly on both sides. Shake off any excess flour.

heat the butter in a large frying pan. Add the floured Dover sole and cook over a gentle heat until they are golden brown on both sides, turning them once.

sprinkle the grated Parmesan over the sole and then cook very gently for another 2–3 minutes until the cheese melts.

add the fish stock and the Marsala or white wine. Cover the pan and cook over a very low heat for 4–5 minutes, until the sole are cooked and tender and the sauce reduced. Serve sprinkled with grated Parmesan and garnish with sprigs of flat leaf parsley and lemon wedges.

Serves 4
Preparation time: *5 minutes*
Cooking time: *12 minutes*

Red Mullet with Tomatoes

6–8 tablespoons olive oil

1 onion, finely chopped

1 garlic clove, crushed

2–3 anchovy fillets, chopped

400 g/13 oz can chopped tomatoes

150 ml/¼ pint dry white wine

1 bay leaf

¼ teaspoon chopped thyme

4 tablespoons plain flour

4 x 175–250 g/6–8 oz red mullet, scales and fins removed

12 black olives, pitted

salt and pepper

thyme sprigs, to garnish

heat 2 tablespoons of the oil in a pan and cook the onion and garlic gently until lightly coloured. Add the anchovy fillets, tomatoes, white wine, bay leaf and thyme. Season to taste and cook gently for about 20 minutes until the sauce thickens.

meanwhile heat 4–6 tablespoons of the oil in a frying pan. Season the flour with salt and pepper, and coat the fish with the flour. Fry until golden brown on one side, then turn carefully and cook on the second side.

add the sauce to the pan with the red mullet and cook for a further 6–8 minutes. Transfer the fish carefully to a warmed serving dish. Toss the olives in the sauce and heat through. Remove the bay leaf and pour the sauce over the fish. Sprinkle the thyme on top and serve hot.

Serves 4
Preparation time: *15–20 minutes*
Cooking time: *30–35 minutes*

clipboard: When scraping the scales from the fish, work from the tail to the head then cut off the fins with a pair of kitchen scissors. Red mullet are usually cooked ungutted.

Grilled Bream
with pesto and tomato sauce

4 red bream steaks or fillets, about 175 g/6 oz each
6 tablespoons olive oil
4 large tomatoes, skinned, deseeded and chopped
4 anchovy fillets, chopped
3 tablespoons Pesto (see page 80)
salt and pepper

To serve
basil sprigs
green salad
crusty bread

season the bream steaks on both sides with salt and pepper and brush with 2 tablespoons of the olive oil.

cook under a preheated grill for 4–5 minutes on each side. Alternatively cook the bream on the greased grill of a preheated barbecue, putting the fish on a special grid if the bars of the barbecue are very wide apart.

meanwhile make the sauce. Heat the remaining 4 tablespoons of olive oil in a pan. Add the tomatoes and anchovy fillets, and salt and pepper to taste (remember that anchovies are very salty). Cook gently for 5 minutes.

stir the pesto sauce into the tomato and anchovy mixture.

put the bream steaks on to a warmed serving dish and spoon over the sauce. Garnish with basil sprigs and serve with a green salad and lots of crusty bread.

Serves 4
Preparation time: *4–5 minutes*
Cooking time: *about 10 minutes*

Octopus and Tomato Salad

Nothing impresses more than tentacles from the sea.

4 tablespoons soy sauce

4 tablespoons Italian salad dressing

50 g/2 oz soft brown sugar

1 kg/2 lb small octopus, cleaned

2 teaspoons olive oil, plus extra for brushing

500 g/1 lb ripe plum tomatoes, cut in half lengthways

1 teaspoon coarse salt

Italian salad dressing

50–75 ml/2–3 fl oz olive oil

2 tablespoons red or white vinegar

1 garlic clove, crushed

salt and pepper

To garnish

dill sprigs

lime wedges

combine the soy sauce, Italian salad dressing and brown sugar in a bowl. Add the octopus and mix to coat. Cover and refrigerate for 1 hour.

brush a baking sheet with olive oil. Place the tomatoes, cut-side up, on the sheet and sprinkle with coarse salt. Drizzle 1 teaspoon of the olive oil over the tomatoes and bake in a preheated oven at 200°C/400°F/Gas Mark 6 for about 10 minutes.

heat the remaining oil in a large frying pan. Drain the octopus and add to the frying pan. Cook the octopus in batches, turning often, on a high heat for 1–2 minutes until just tender but cooked.

serve the octopus in a large bowl with the roasted tomatoes. Garnish the dish with dill sprigs and lime wedges.

Serves 6
Preparation time: *20 minutes, plus marinating*
Cooking time: *about 12 minutes*
Oven temperature: *200°C/400°F/Gas Mark 6*

Pasta & Gnocchi

Fresh Pasta
is quite simple to make at home

300 g/10 oz strong plain bread flour, sifted

pinch of salt

3 eggs

1 tablespoon olive oil

flour, for dusting

place the flour and a pinch of salt on a work surface. Make a well in the centre and add the eggs. Using your fingertips, draw the flour in from the sides and mix well. Add the olive oil and continue mixing until you have a soft dough. Alternatively, make the dough in a food processor.

turn out the dough on to a lightly floured surface and knead well until it is really smooth and silky. Roll out the dough, giving it an occasional quarter-turn and stretching it out, until it resembles a thin sheet of cloth and is almost transparent.

hang the pasta over the back of a chair, a broom handle or a pasta stand and leave for about 10 minutes to dry. Alternatively, lay it on a table with one-third overhanging the edge and keep turning it so that it dries out completely.

roll up the pasta loosely like a Swiss roll and then cut through horizontally at regular intervals to make fettuccine (3 mm/⅛ inch wide) or tagliatelle (5 mm/¼ inch wide). Unravel them and toss gently in a little flour. Leave them to dry on a cloth for at least 30 minutes before cooking in a large pan of lightly salted boiling water until tender but firm to the bite. Serve tossed with olive oil, garlic, salt and pepper and parsley, or with the pasta sauce of your choice.

Serves 4
Preparation time: *1 hour*
Cooking time: *2–3 minutes*

clipboard: To make lasagne or ravioli, cut the pasta into sheets rather than strips.

Tagliatelle al Sugo di Pomodoro

375 g/12 oz dried tagliatelle
1 teaspoon vegetable oil
1 tablespoon olive oil
50 g/2 oz Parmesan cheese shavings, to serve

Tomato Sauce

3 tablespoons olive oil
2 onions, chopped
2 garlic cloves, crushed
500 g/1 lb plum tomatoes, skinned and chopped
2 tablespoons tomato purée
1 teaspoon sugar
125 ml/4 fl oz dry white wine
few ripe olives, pitted and quartered
2–3 tablespoons torn basil leaves
salt and pepper

first make the tomato sauce. Heat the olive oil in a large frying pan. Add the onions and garlic, and sauté gently over a low heat until they are tender and lightly coloured, stirring the mixture occasionally.

add the tomatoes and tomato purée together with the sugar and wine, stirring well. Cook over a low heat until the mixture is quite thick and reduced. Stir in the olives and basil leaves and season to taste with salt and plenty of pepper.

meanwhile, cook the tagliatelle with the vegetable oil in a large pan of salted boiling water until the pasta is tender but firm to the bite.

drain the tagliatelle immediately, mixing in the olive oil and seasoning well with pepper. Arrange the pasta on 4 warmed serving plates and top with the tomato sauce, stirring it into the tagliatelle. Serve sprinkled with Parmesan shavings.

Serves 4
Preparation time: *10 minutes*
Cooking time: *20 minutes*

Fusilli with Aubergines

and tomato and bacon sauce

1 large aubergine, diced
125–150 ml/4 fl oz–¼ pint olive oil
500 g/1 lb dried fusilli
1 quantity Tomato and Bacon Sauce (see clipboard, below)
salt and pepper
basil sprigs and leaves, to serve

put the aubergine into a colander and sprinkle with salt. Leave for at least 30 minutes to drain. This will remove some of the bitter juices from the aubergines. Rinse thoroughly, drain well and dry on kitchen paper.

heat half of the oil in a frying pan and cook some of the aubergine dice until golden brown. Repeat, adding more oil to the pan if necessary until all the aubergine is cooked. Keep hot.

cook the fusilli in a large pan of lightly salted boiling water for about 12 minutes until tender but firm to the bite. Drain well and stir into the hot sauce. Check the seasoning and add salt and pepper to taste. Turn into a serving bowl and put the fried aubergine on top. Serve sprinkled with basil sprigs and leaves.

Serves 4
Preparation time: *20 minutes, plus draining*
Cooking time: *40–45 minutes*

clipboard: To make the Tomato and Bacon Sauce, gently fry 1 chopped onion, 2 crushed garlic cloves and 2 chopped rashers of streaky bacon in 1–2 tablespoons of olive oil. When soft, add a 400g/13 oz can chopped tomatoes, and season. Simmer for 25–30 minutes until thickened. For a smooth sauce, liquidize then sieve to remove the seeds.

Tagliatelle al Pesto

500 g/1 lb tagliatelle

salt and pepper

50 g/2 oz Parmesan cheese, grated, to serve

Pesto

50 g/2 oz pine nuts

1 garlic clove, crushed

50 g/2 oz basil leaves

75 g/3 oz Parmesan cheese, grated

juice of ½ lemon

125 ml/4 fl oz olive oil

to make the pesto, spread the pine nuts on a baking sheet and place in a preheated oven at 220°C/425°F/Gas Mark 7 for 3–5 minutes, until golden. Keep checking them to make sure that they do not burn.

pound the pine nuts with the garlic to a thick paste using a pestle and mortar. Alternatively, use a food processor or blender.

tear the basil leaves into shreds and add to the pine nut mixture. Continue pounding or processing until you have a thick green paste. Transfer to a bowl (if using a mortar) and stir in the grated Parmesan and lemon juice. Add the olive oil, a little at a time, beating well in between each addition.

cook the tagliatelle in a large pan of salted boiling water until tender but firm to the bite; drain well. Sprinkle with pepper and toss the pasta lightly with the pesto sauce. Serve sprinkled with Parmesan.

Serves 4
Preparation time: *15–20 minutes*
Cooking time: *5–12 minutes*
Oven temperature:
  220°C/425°F/Gas Mark 7

Fusilli with Anchovies and Olives

1 teaspoon vegetable oil
375 g/12 oz dried fusilli
25 g/1 oz butter
6 anchovy fillets, chopped
1 tablespoon tomato purée
1 tablespoon olive paste
6 pitted black olives, chopped
handful of basil leaves
salt and pepper
grated Parmesan cheese, to garnish

bring a large pan of salted water to the boil. Add the oil. Cook the pasta for 8–12 minutes or according to packet instructions, until just tender but firm to the bite.

drain the pasta and set it aside. Melt the butter in a large saucepan. Add the anchovy fillets, tomato purée, olive paste and olives. Stir over the heat until the mixture sizzles. Season well with pepper. Cool for 1 minute.

add the drained pasta to the saucepan and toss well. Tear the basil leaves into pieces and add them to the pasta. Serve immediately, garnished with grated Parmesan.

Serves 4
Preparation time: *10 minutes*
Cooking time: *about 15 minutes*

Fresh & Dry Pasta

Fusilli verdi

Tortellini

Assorted fiorelli

Conchiglie

Farfalle

Fusilli verdi

Fusilli means twists or corkscrews. Because they are virtually made of ridges, fusilli are one of the shapes that hold a lot of sauce. They are shown above coloured green with spinach. Water can be held in the fusilli ridges so extra care is needed when draining them.

Conchiglie

These are shell-shaped pasta – their name translates as little shells or conches. They come in various sizes and may have a smooth surface or a ribbed texture (*rigate*), as shown here. Conchiglie go well with minced meat sauces. As with fusilli, special care is needed when draining them.

Tortellini

Tortellini are a small version of tortelli, a stuffed pasta shape which originated in Bologna. Spinach and ricotta is a favourite filling for tortellini; they are sold ready-filled or you can make your own. Like ravioli, they are served with a sauce or with melted butter and grated Parmesan.

Farfalle

The name of this small shape translates as bows or butterflies, and it is available in a variety of sizes. Fresh and dried farfalle, and other pastas, have a different cooking time, and pasta produced by different manufacturers can also vary, so always read the packet instructions carefully before starting to cook.

Assorted fiorelli

The name of this pretty little pasta shape means flower. It is sold in packets of mixed colours – white, green and red – the Italian national colours. Green pasta is coloured with spinach, red with tomatoes. Also available, but not so easy to find, are black, coloured with squid ink and brown, with mushrooms.

Spaghetti

Fresh tagliatelle

Lasagne verdi

Penne

Pappardelle

Spaghetti

The classic pasta, and possibly the universal favourite, spaghetti may be fresh or dried, the dried form including a wholemeal version. Other long strings or ribbons of pasta include *tagliatelle*, *spaghettini* (a very thin type of spaghetti), *fusilli lunghi* (an elongated corkscrew shape), *taglionini* and *fettuccine*.

Penne

The name of this short tubular-shaped pasta means quills, recalling the quill pens of olden times. Penne may be smooth or with a ridged surface. Among the many other small pasta shapes are *lumache* (snail shells), *ditali* (thimbles) *orecciette* (ears), *ruoti* (wheels) and *capelleti* (little hats).

Tagliatelle

The fresh egg tagliatelle shown above is coiled into nests. Tagliatelle, which came originally from Bologna, is flat ribbon pasta and so technically a noodle. The combination of green and yellow tagliatelle is known as *paglio e fieno* or hay and straw noodles. It is also available dried.

Pappardelle

This is a wide ribbon noodle, sometimes made even more distinctive by a crinkly edge. Like tagliatelle, it can be found coiled into nests.

Lasagne verdi

Lasagne is made in broad flat sheets which may be fresh or dried. The sheets are usually cooked layered with meat, cheese, vegetables and a sauce, or sauces, and baked in the oven. A dish made with a combination of plain and green lasagne can look very effective. Cannelloni are sometimes made with sheets of lasagne.

Spaghetti alla Vongole

2 litres/3½ pints fresh clams
150 ml/¼ pint dry white wine
2 tablespoons olive oil
3 garlic cloves, finely chopped
750 g/1½ lb tomatoes, skinned and chopped
500 g/1 lb spaghetti or spaghettini
1 teaspoon vegetable oil
2 tablespoons chopped flat leaf parsley
salt and pepper

scrub the clams under cold running water to remove all sand and grit. Discard any that do not close when tapped. Put the clams into a saucepan, add the wine, cover and cook for 5 minutes. Strain, reserving the liquid. Remove the clams from their shells, discarding any that have not opened, and leaving a few in their half shells for garnish.

heat the oil in a saucepan and fry the garlic until just golden. Add the tomatoes and simmer gently for 10 minutes.

cook the spaghetti with the vegetable oil in a large pan of lightly salted boiling water for 8–12 minutes, or according to the packet instructions, until tender but firm to the bite.

meanwhile add the clams, the strained cooking liquid and parsley to the tomato mixture and season to taste. Cook gently for 5 minutes to heat through. Drain the pasta thoroughly and mix with the sauce over a gentle heat. Transfer to a warmed serving dish and serve immediately.

Serves 4–6
Preparation time: *20 minutes*
Cooking time: *25–30 minutes*

Mushroom and Mozzarella Lasagne Stacks

2 tablespoons olive oil
50 g/2 oz butter
2 onions, chopped
2 garlic cloves, chopped
500 g/1 lb mushrooms, trimmed and sliced
4 tablespoons double cream
4 tablespoons dry white wine
1 teaspoon chopped thyme
8 pieces dried lasagne
1 tablespoon vegetable oil
2 red peppers, skinned (see page 30) cored, deseeded and thickly sliced
125 g/4 oz young spinach leaves
125 g/4 oz packet mozzarella cheese
salt and pepper
50 g/2 oz Parmesan cheese shavings

heat the oil and butter in a saucepan, add the onions and sauté for 3 minutes. Add the garlic and cook for 1 minute.

add the mushrooms, turn up the heat and cook for 5 minutes. Add the cream, white wine and thyme, season with salt and pepper and simmer for 4 minutes.

bring a pan of water to the boil, add the lasagne sheets a few pieces at a time and the vegetable oil, and cook for 7 minutes or according to packet instructions until tender but firm to the bite. Remove from the pan and place 4 pieces in a well-oiled large ovenproof dish.

place a generous spoonful of mushroom mixture on each piece of lasagne, add some red pepper slices and half of the spinach and place another piece of lasagne on top. Then add the remaining spinach, a little more mushroom mixture and top with a slice of mozzarella. Finish with the Parmesan shavings. Place the dish under a preheated very hot grill and cook for 5 minutes until the Parmesan is bubbling.

Serves 4
Preparation time: *10 minutes*
Cooking time: *20 minutes*

Ravioli di Spinaci e Ricotta

1 quantity Fresh Pasta Dough (see page 74)

Filling
250 g/8 oz spinach
125 g/4 oz fresh ricotta cheese
25 g/1 oz Parmesan cheese, grated
grated nutmeg
1 egg, beaten
salt and pepper

To serve
50 g/2 oz butter, melted
3–4 sage leaves, torn
Parmesan cheese, grated

first make the filling. Wash the spinach, place it in a saucepan with just the water that clings to the leaves and heat gently for 3–4 minutes until wilted. Drain the spinach in a colander, pressing out all the moisture, then chop it roughly.

place the ricotta and Parmesan in a bowl and mix in the chopped spinach. Add the grated nutmeg and beaten egg, season with salt and pepper and mix well to a paste.

roll out the pasta as thinly as possible on a lightly floured surface and cut into 2 equal pieces. Place teaspoons of the ricotta and spinach filling over one piece of pasta at regular intervals, about 5 cm/2 inches apart.

cover with the other sheet of pasta and press gently around each little mound with your fingers. Using a pastry cutter wheel, cut the pasta into squares, each containing a mound of filling. Cook the ravioli in a large pan of gently boiling water for 4–5 minutes, until they rise to the surface. Drain and serve with melted butter, sprinkled with sage and Parmesan.

Serves 4–6
Preparation time: *25 minutes*
Cooking time: *10 minutes*

Spinach and Ricotta Gnocchi

These delicate gnocchi are piped straight into a pan of boiling water, making them quicker and easier to prepare than potato gnocchi.

125 g/4 oz frozen spinach, thawed
250 g/8 oz ricotta cheese
2 small eggs, beaten
50 g/2 oz Parmesan cheese, grated
1 tablespoon chopped basil
50 g/2 oz plain flour
salt and pepper
Parmesan cheese, grated, to serve

Sauce
50 g/2 oz unsalted butter
1 garlic clove, crushed
1 red chilli, deseeded and chopped

squeeze out the excess water from the spinach and chop finely. Place in a food processor or blender with the ricotta and process until smooth. Beat in the eggs, Parmesan and basil, salt and pepper to taste, and enough flour to form a soft, slightly sticky dough.

bring a large pan of salted water to the boil. Transfer the spinach mixture to a piping bag fitted with a large plain nozzle. As soon as the water is boiling, pipe about 12 short lengths of gnocchi into the water, using a sharp knife to cut away from the nozzle as you pipe.

cook the gnocchi for 2–3 minutes until they rise to the surface, then remove with a slotted spoon, drain on kitchen paper and transfer to a warmed serving dish. Keep warm while cooking the remaining gnocchi.

to make the sauce, melt the butter in a small pan and fry the garlic and chilli for 2 minutes. Pour over the gnocchi and toss well. Sprinkle with Parmesan and serve at once.

Serves 4
Preparation time: *20 minutes*
Cooking time: *12–15 minutes*

Beef, Lamb & Pork

Bresaolo

Salami Milanese

Mortadella

Pancetta

cuitto di Parma

Salami Napoli

Bocconcino

Salami Milanese

This is one the best known Italian salamis and exported widely all over the world. It is also known as *crespone* and is a finely minced pork salami flavoured with garlic which has been crushed in red wine.

Salami Napoli

Another well-known and widely available sausage, Neapolitan salami is made with a combination of pork, beef and pork fat. A coarsely ground salami, it is generously spiced with chilli and garlic.

Mortadella

The best known of all the Italian slicing sausages, mortadella is a large lightly smoked sausage made of finely minced pork or a mixture of meats. It is seasoned with parsley and studded with olives, pistachio nuts and small cubes of fat.

Bocconcino

These are small, sausage-shaped salamis which are sold in a string. They are made of raw pork or other red meat interspersed with fat and are very highly seasoned. Bocconcino should be sliced finely and eaten in salads or in sandwiches.

Pancetta

This is unsmoked bacon taken from the belly of the pig. It is cured with spices, salt and pepper. The bacon is then rolled into a sausage shape and sliced very thinly. Pancetta is also diced and used as a flavouring in soups and stews.

Calves' Liver Venetian-style

6 tablespoons olive oil
1 tablespoon butter
4 onions, thinly sliced
625 g/1¼ lb calves' liver, thinly sliced
4 tablespoons Chicken Stock (see page 10)
1 tablespoon wine vinegar
2 tablespoons finely chopped parsley
salt and pepper

heat the olive oil with the butter in a large heavy-based frying pan. Add the onions and cook gently over a very low heat, stirring occasionally, for about 40 minutes, or until the onions are soft, golden and translucent but not browned. Remove the onions with a slotted spoon and keep warm.

add the thinly sliced calves' liver to the pan and fry very quickly until brown on one side. Turn over and quickly cook the other side. The liver should be lightly browned on the outside and still pink in the middle. Remove and keep warm.

add the chicken stock and vinegar to the pan and bring to the boil, scraping the bottom of the pan with a wooden spoon to pick up the juices from the liver and stirring until the sauce reduces. Season to taste with salt and pepper, and stir in the chopped parsley.

arrange the liver and onions on a heated serving dish or 4 warmed serving plates, and pour the sauce over the top. Serve with a bowl of fresh pasta and a crisp green salad.

Serves 4
Preparation time: *10 minutes*
Cooking time: *1¼ hours*

La Fiorentina

This must be one of Tuscany's most famous dishes. It is unbelievably simple to make, but it does need good quality steak. In this recipe a thick cut of sirloin is used instead of the usual T-bone. Here it is cooked on a barbecue, but use a grill if you prefer.

1 sirloin steak, 2.5–4 cm/1–1½ inches thick
about 2 tablespoons olive oil
salt and pepper
salad leaves, to serve

prepare the barbecue and let it burn until all the flames have died down and the coals have turned grey.

put the steak on the barbecue grill and cook for 5 minutes, then turn the steak over and sprinkle the cooked side with salt and pepper. Cook for a further 5 minutes, turn again and sprinkle the second cooked side with salt and pepper. Cook for 2 minutes.

remove the steak from the barbecue grill and sprinkle with olive oil. Serve immediately with salad leaves.

Serves 1
Preparation time: *1–2 minutes, plus preparing the barbecue*
Cooking time: *12 minutes*

clipboard: *La Fiorentina* is traditionally served very rare, and the cooking time given here is for rare steak, but you can cook the meat longer if you prefer.

Beef Steaks Pizzaiolo

75 ml/3 fl oz olive oil
1–2 garlic cloves, crushed
500 g/1 lb tomatoes, peeled and chopped, or
400 g/13 oz can chopped tomatoes
1 teaspoon chopped oregano
4 x 250 g/8 oz thinly cut beef steaks, trimmed of
all fat
salt and pepper
oregano sprigs, to garnish

heat three-quarters of the oil in a saucepan and cook the garlic gently until golden brown. Add the tomatoes, season lightly with salt and pepper and add the oregano. Bring to the boil and simmer for 10–15 minutes, until the sauce thickens slightly.

meanwhile heat the remaining oil in a frying pan and quickly brown the meat on both sides. Pour the tomato sauce over and continue cooking very gently for 10–15 minutes, or until the meat is tender. If necessary, add a little water to prevent the sauce reducing too much.

arrange the steaks on warmed individual plates or a serving dish and pour the sauce over. Garnish with oregano sprigs and serve immediately.

Serves 4
Preparation time: *15–20 minutes*
Cooking time: *25–35 minutes*

clipboard: This dish gets its name because it is cooked like a pizza with a topping of tomatoes, garlic and oregano. It is a very good recipe to use for steaks which are not very tender, or with pork chops. Simmer very gently until they tenderize, taking care that the sauce never boils as this would toughen the meat.

Stuffed Beef Olives

1 kg/2 lb beef topside
125 g/4 oz pecorino cheese, grated
2 slices Parma ham, chopped
3 garlic cloves, crushed
3 tablespoons chopped parsley
1 tablespoon chopped basil
3 tablespoons olive oil
salt and pepper
few basil leaves, to garnish

Tomato Sauce
1 onion, chopped
2 garlic cloves, crushed
1 kg/2 lb tomatoes, skinned and chopped
1 tablespoon tomato purée
125 ml/4 fl oz red wine

cut the beef into thin slices and place between 2 sheets of greaseproof paper. Flatten them with a rolling pin and then season on both sides with salt and pepper.

to make the filling, place the grated pecorino in a bowl with the chopped ham, garlic, parsley and basil. Mix well together and spread a little of this mixture on to each slice of beef. Roll up, folding in the sides, and secure with cotton or fine string.

heat the olive oil in a large saucepan and gently fry the beef olives until they are lightly browned all over, turning as necessary. Remove from the pan and keep warm.

to make the sauce, add the onion and garlic to the oil in the pan and sauté until soft. Add the tomatoes, tomato purée, wine and salt and pepper to taste. Bring to the boil, and then add the beef olives. Cover and simmer gently for 1½–2 hours, or until tender. Remove the string from the beef olives and serve with the sauce, sprinkled with basil.

Serves 6
Preparation time: *20 minutes*
Cooking time: *1¾–2¼ hours*

Pork, Ham and Sage Rolls

50 g/2 oz sultanas

4 tablespoons Marsala

4 long thin pork steaks (cut from the tenderloin),
about 75 g/3 oz each

4 thick slices Parma ham

1 tablespoon chopped sage

16 cubes white bread, about 2.5 cm/1 inch square

4 tablespoons olive oil

8 thin slices bacon, rinded and halved crossways

salt and pepper

mix the sultanas with the Marsala. Cover and leave to stand for 1 hour.

cut each pork steak into 4 long strips, then cut the slices of ham into strips roughly the same size.

lay a strip of ham on top of each strip of pork. Sprinkle each strip with some chopped sage, a few of the sultanas, and salt and pepper to taste. Roll each strip up neatly, so that you have 16 sausage shapes.

brush each cube of bread with a little olive oil, then roll each one in half a bacon slice.

thread 4 pork and ham rolls and 4 bread and bacon rolls alternately on to each of 4 kebab skewers. Brush the kebabs with olive oil.

cook on the greased grill of a preheated barbecue or under a preheated grill for 3–4 minutes on each side. Serve hot with a green salad.

Serves 4
Preparation time: *30 minutes,*
 plus standing
Cooking time: *7–8 minutes*

Sausages
with beans and sage

*Ask at your Italian delicatessen for fresh pork sausages —
salsiccia puro suino. There are many different kinds but
whichever you choose, they are bound to have a high meat
content because this is how Italians like their sausages.*

250 g/8 oz dried cannellini beans, soaked overnight
5 tablespoons olive oil
500 g/1 lb Italian pork sausages, chopped
250 ml/8 fl oz passata (Italian sieved tomatoes)
2 garlic cloves, crushed
1 sage sprig
salt and pepper
sage leaves, to garnish

drain the beans and rinse under cold running water. Place them in a
large saucepan, cover with water and bring to the boil. Boil rapidly for
10 minutes, then lower the heat and half cover with a lid. Simmer for
1¼ hours or until the beans are tender, skimming off the scum and
topping up the water level as necessary. Drain the beans and reserve the
cooking liquid.

heat 3 tablespoons of the oil in a large flameproof casserole, add the
sausages and cook over a moderate heat until browned on all sides. Add
the passata, garlic, sage and salt and pepper to taste and stir well to mix.
Bring to the boil, then add the beans and a few spoonfuls of the cooking
liquid. Cover and simmer, stirring frequently, for 15 minutes — the
consistency should be quite thick. Taste for seasoning.

drizzle the remaining olive oil over the dish and serve garnished with
fresh sage leaves.

Serves 4
Preparation time: *15 minutes,
  plus soaking*
Cooking time: *about 1¾ hours*

Veal Chops with Gremolata

75 g/3 oz plain flour
4 thin veal chops
50 g/2 oz butter
1 tablespoon olive oil
2 onions, chopped
2 garlic cloves, crushed and chopped
2 celery sticks, chopped
1 carrot, chopped
2 bay leaves
6 tomatoes, skinned, deseeded and chopped
125 ml/4 fl oz Chicken Stock (see page 10)
125 ml/4 fl oz dry white wine
salt and pepper

Gremolata
2 tablespoons finely chopped parsley
1 tablespoon finely chopped sage
finely grated rind of 3 lemons
3 large garlic cloves, chopped

season the flour with salt and pepper and coat both sides of the veal chops. Melt the butter and oil in a large flameproof casserole, add the chops and brown well on each side. Remove the chops from the casserole and keep them warm.

add the onions, garlic, celery and carrot to the casserole and sauté, stirring, for 3 minutes.

add the bay leaves, tomatoes, stock, wine and salt and pepper, mix well and bring to the boil. Return the chops to the casserole and turn to coat them thoroughly in the sauce. Cover and cook in a preheated oven at 200°C/400°F/Gas Mark 6 for 20 minutes.

meanwhile, make the gremolata. Mix together the parsley, sage, lemon rind and garlic.

transfer the chops to a warmed serving platter and keep them warm. Boil the sauce to reduce if necessary, remove the bay leaves, then pour the sauce over the chops. Spoon some of the gremolata over each one and serve.

Serves 4
Preparation time: *10 minutes*
Cooking time: *35 minutes*
Oven temperature:
  200°C/400°F/Gas Mark 6

Veal Scaloppine al Basilico

16 small veal escalopes
3 tablespoons flour
1 basil sprig
2 garlic cloves
75 g/3 oz butter
125 ml/4 fl oz dry white wine
125 ml/4 fl oz water
salt and pepper
basil sprigs, to garnish

flatten the escalopes with a dampened meat mallet and coat lightly in the flour. Strip the leaves from the basil and chop together roughly with the garlic cloves.

melt two-thirds of the butter in a large shallow pan over a moderate heat until foaming. Add the veal and cook for 1–2 minutes on each side then remove from the pan, set aside and keep warm. Add the wine and water to the pan and season with salt and pepper. Bring to the boil then reduce the heat and cook about 10 minutes, until the sauce is thick and smooth.

transfer the escalopes to a warmed serving dish. Add the remaining butter to the pan, then the basil and garlic mixture. Cook, stirring, for about 1 minute, and pour over the veal. Serve accompanied by courgettes or a green salad.

Serves 8
Preparation time: *15 minutes*
Cooking time: *15–20 minutes*

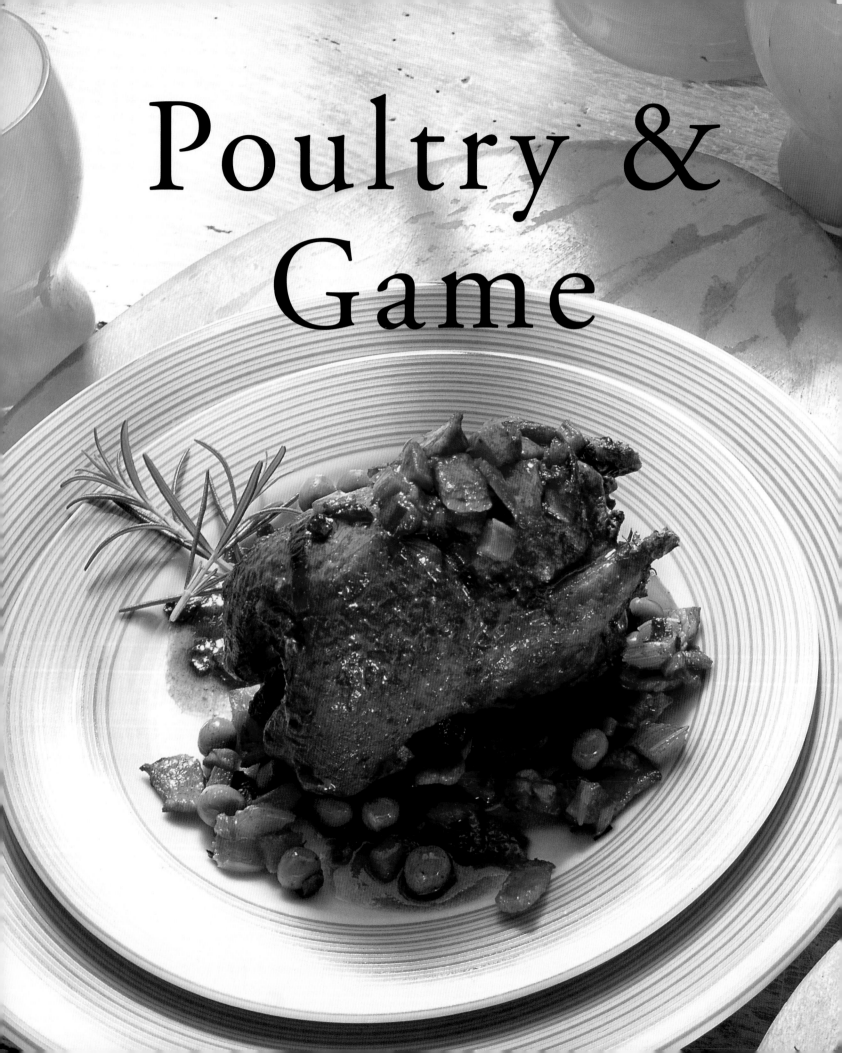

Poultry & Game

Stuffed Chicken Breasts

4 boneless skinless chicken breasts
4 thin small slices Parma ham
4 thin slices Bel Paese cheese
4 cooked or canned asparagus spears
flour, for dusting
50 g/2 oz butter
1 tablespoon olive oil
6 tablespoons Marsala or dry white wine
2 tablespoons Chicken Stock (see page 10)
salt and pepper
flat leaf parsley sprigs, to garnish

place each chicken breast between 2 sheets of greaseproof paper and beat until thin. Season lightly with salt and pepper.

put a slice of Parma ham on top of each chicken breast, then a slice of Bel Paese and, finally, an asparagus spear. Roll each breast up and wind a piece of cotton around to hold it. Tie securely and dust with flour.

heat 25 g/1 oz of the butter with the oil in a frying pan. Sauté the chicken rolls over a very low heat, turning them frequently, for about 15 minutes, or until tender, cooked and golden. Remove the cotton, and transfer the rolls to a serving dish and keep warm.

add the Marsala or wine, chicken stock and the remaining butter to the juices in the pan. Bring to the boil and simmer for 3–4 minutes, scraping the base of the pan with a wooden spoon to pick up all the juices. Spoon the sauce over the chicken, garnish with parsley sprigs and serve with asparagus spears, if liked.

Serves 4
Preparation time: *20 minutes*
Cooking time: *about 30 minutes*

Chicken Cacciatore

3–4 tablespoons olive oil
1.5 kg/3 lb chicken, jointed
50 g/2 oz fat bacon, diced
1 onion, finely chopped
1 garlic clove, crushed
1 teaspoon flour
150 ml/¼ pint dry white wine
300 ml/½ pint Chicken Stock (see page 10)
4 ripe tomatoes, skinned, deseeded and sliced
1 teaspoon tomato purée
125 g/4 oz mushrooms, quartered
salt and pepper
chopped flat-leaf parsley and parsley sprigs, to serve

heat 2 tablespoons of the oil in a casserole and brown the chicken pieces on all sides. Remove from the pan and add the bacon. Cook until golden brown, then remove from the pan. Add more oil if necessary and cook the onion and garlic gently until golden brown. Add the flour and cook together for a few moments, then stir in the white wine, stock, tomatoes and tomato purée. Bring to the boil and season lightly.

return the chicken and bacon to the casserole. Cover tightly and cook in a preheated oven at 190°C/375°F/Gas Mark 5 for 25–30 minutes. Add the mushrooms and continue cooking for a further 10–15 minutes until the chicken and mushrooms are tender.

put the chicken pieces on a warmed serving dish, cover and keep warm. If necessary, boil the sauce to reduce it to a coating consistency. Pour the sauce over the chicken, sprinkle with the parsley and garnish with the parsley sprigs just before serving.

Serves 4
Preparation time: *25–30 minutes*
Cooking time: *about 1 hour*
Oven temperature:
  190°C/375°F/Gas Mark 5

clipboard: You can use 4 chicken breasts or 8 thighs for this recipe. Chicken breasts will only need a total of 25–30 minutes to cook but thighs will need longer.

Tuscan Chicken
with polenta

4 tablespoons olive oil
1 chicken, jointed
1 onion, chopped
5 plum tomatoes, skinned and chopped
300 ml/½ pint dry white wine
1 rosemary sprig
1 tablespoon chopped thyme
15 g/½ oz flour
15 g/½ oz butter
salt and pepper
2 tablespoons chopped parsley, to serve

Polenta
1.8 litres/3 pints water
300 g/10 oz instant polenta flour
15 g/½ oz butter

heat the olive oil in a large heavy-based frying pan and sauté the chicken joints until golden brown all over, turning occasionally. Remove from the pan and keep warm.

add the onion to the pan and cook gently until soft and golden. Add the chopped tomatoes, white wine, rosemary, thyme and salt and pepper to taste. Bring to the boil, stirring, and then reduce the heat to a simmer. Return the chicken to the pan and then simmer, covered, for 20–30 minutes until the chicken is cooked.

meanwhile, make the polenta. Heat the water to a gentle simmer, pour in the polenta flour and beat well for 1–2 minutes until it is a smooth paste. Turn the heat down and continue to cook the polenta until it thickens, stirring constantly, for 6–8 minutes until it is thick and smooth and has absorbed all the liquid. Stir in the butter and season with salt and pepper.

remove the chicken and arrange on a warmed serving dish. Blend the flour and butter (*beurre manié*) and add to the sauce. Bring to the boil, stirring constantly, until the sauce thickens slightly. Pour the sauce over the chicken, sprinkle with parsley and serve with the polenta.

Serves 4
Preparation time: *15 minutes*
Cooking time: *40 minutes*

Pollo alla Valdostana

6 part-boned chicken breasts
½ teaspoon dried oregano
½ teaspoon dried basil
2 tablespoons olive oil
3 slices Parma ham
2 garlic cloves, crushed
2 tablespoons balsamic vinegar
6 tablespoons dry Italian vermouth or dry white wine
3 thin slices Fontina cheese, about 75 g/3 oz in total
salt and pepper
basil sprigs, to garnish

sprinkle the opening in each chicken breast with the dried oregano and basil and add salt and pepper to taste.

heat the oil in a large sauté pan. Add the chicken breasts and sauté over a moderate heat for 1–2 minutes on each side until they just change colour. Remove with a slotted spoon and leave until cool enough to handle. Reserve the oil.

cut the slices of Parma ham in half. Stuff each chicken breast with a piece of ham, then place the chicken breasts in a single layer in a lightly oiled ovenproof dish.

return the pan to the heat, add the garlic and balsamic vinegar and stir until sizzling. Stir in the vermouth or wine and pour over the chicken breasts. Halve each slice of Fontina, and place a slice on top of each chicken breast.

put the chicken in a preheated oven at 200°C/400°F/Gas Mark 6 and cook for 20 minutes or until the Fontina melts and the chicken is tender. Season with pepper and serve garnished with basil.

Serves 6
Preparation time: *15 minutes*
Cooking time: *about 25 minutes*
Oven temperature:
   200°C/400°F/Gas Mark 6

Pot-roast Turkey

3 kg/6 lb oven-ready turkey, giblets removed
2 tablespoons olive oil
15 g/½ oz butter
4 tablespoons anise-flavoured liqueur
150 ml/¼ pint dry white wine
salt and pepper

Risotto Stuffing
2 tablespoons olive oil
1 onion, finely chopped
125 g/4 oz arborio rice
900 ml/1½ pints hot Chicken Stock (see page 10)
125 g/4 oz rindless pancetta, chopped
1 fennel bulb, finely chopped, with fronds reserved
2 garlic cloves, finely chopped
50 g/2 oz grated Parmesan cheese
1 egg, beaten

first make the stuffing. Heat the oil in a saucepan and gently fry the onion, stirring, until soft. Stir in the rice, add half of the stock and bring to the boil. Stir until the stock is absorbed, then add the remaining stock and return to the boil. Cover and simmer, stirring frequently, for 15 minutes or until all the stock is absorbed. Set aside.

fry the pancetta until the fat starts to run. Add the fennel, garlic and pepper to taste and cook, stirring, for 10 minutes until soft. Add to the rice with half of the Parmesan and the egg. Stir, then leave to cool.

fill the neck end of the turkey with the stuffing, and truss with string. Place any leftover stuffing in an oiled baking dish and sprinkle with the remaining Parmesan. Heat the oil with the butter in a large flameproof casserole. Add the turkey and cook for about 10 minutes until lightly coloured on all sides. Pour the liqueur over the turkey, allow to sizzle, then pour over the wine and season to taste.

cover and cook in a preheated oven at 180°C/350°F/Gas Mark 4 for 2½–3 hours until the juices run clear when the thickest part of a thigh is pierced with a skewer or sharp knife. Baste occasionally. Place the dish of stuffing in the oven for the last 15–20 minutes, until heated through.

remove the bird from the oven, and discard the trussing string. Cover tightly with foil and set aside to rest for about 15 minutes. Keep the cooking juices hot. Serve the turkey garnished with the reserved fennel fronds, with the cooking juices and any extra stuffing handed separately.

Serves 6–8
Preparation time: *30 minutes, plus standing*
Cooking time: *3–3½ hours*
Oven temperature: *180°C/350°F/Gas Mark 4*

Guinea Fowl
with mushrooms and gnocchi

1 plump guinea fowl, cut into 8 pieces

2 tablespoons seasoned flour

2 tablespoons olive oil

2 shallots, finely chopped

1 garlic clove, crushed

2 tablespoons chopped sage

250 ml/8 fl oz dry white wine

250 ml/8 fl oz Chicken Stock (see page 10)

1 bay leaf

salt and pepper

Gnocchi

750 g/1½ lb large potatoes, unpeeled

1 egg, beaten

3 tablespoons chopped parsley

125 g/4 oz plain flour, sifted

Mushrooms

50 g/2 oz butter

1 shallot, finely chopped

500 g/1 lb mixed wild or cultivated mushrooms, cut into halves or quarters if large

finely grated rind of 1 lemon

2 tablespoons lemon juice

roll the guinea fowl in the seasoned flour, shaking off any excess. Heat the oil in a large flameproof casserole, add the guinea fowl, in batches, and brown well all over. Remove with a slotted spoon and set aside. Reduce the heat, add the shallots, garlic and sage and cook gently for 5 minutes until soft. Add the wine and bring to the boil, scraping up any residue from the bottom of the casserole. Return the guinea fowl and add the stock and bay leaf. Bring back to the boil, reduce the heat, cover and simmer gently for 25–30 minutes.

meanwhile make the gnocchi. Boil the potatoes, drain well and peel. While still warm, press through a sieve into a bowl. Beat the egg and parsley into the potato mixture. Add the flour a little at a time (you may not need it all) until the mixture is smooth and slightly sticky. Season with salt. Roll out on a lightly floured surface to form a long sausage 1 cm/½ inch in diameter. Cut into 1.5 cm/¾ inch lengths. Take one piece at a time and press it on to a floured fork. Roll along the prongs and off the fork on to a floured tray. Set aside.

to cook the mushrooms, melt the butter in a pan over a low heat, add the shallot and cook until soft. Add the mushrooms, lemon rind and juice and cook until soft. Stir into the casserole for the last 10 minutes of cooking.

drop 20–25 pieces of gnocchi at a time into a large pan of boiling water. They will quickly rise to the surface. Cook for 10–15 seconds. Remove with a slotted spoon, drain and keep warm while cooking the remainder. Discard the bay leaf, and serve the casserole with the gnocchi.

Serves 4

Preparation time: *45 minutes*

Cooking time: *about 1 hour*

Braised Pheasant
with Marsala and chestnuts

500 g/1 lb fresh chestnuts or 250 g/8 oz vacuum-
packed cooked chestnuts
25 g/1 oz butter
1–1.25 kg/2–2½ lb pheasant
125 g/4 oz pancetta or streaky bacon, cut into strips
1 large onion, chopped
1 celery stick, chopped
1 large carrot, chopped
1 tablespoon chopped sage
125 ml/4 fl oz Marsala
500 ml/17 fl oz game stock or Chicken Stock (see
page 10)
salt and pepper

Beetroot straws
250 g/8 oz raw beetroot
oil, for deep-frying

cut a slash in the pointed end of each fresh chestnut, if using. Place the chestnuts in a saucepan, cover with water, bring to the boil and simmer for 2 minutes. Remove the pan from the heat. Using a slotted spoon, take out one chestnut at a time and remove the outer and inner skins.

melt the butter in a large flameproof casserole over a moderate heat, brown the pheasant all over, then transfer the bird to a plate. Reduce the heat, add the pancetta or streaky bacon and cook for 1 minute. Add the onion, celery and carrot and cook until the onion has softened.

return the pheasant to the pan and add the sage, Marsala and stock, and the fresh chestnuts, if using. Season, bring to the boil, cover and simmer gently for 35–45 minutes until the pheasant and chestnuts are cooked. If using cooked chestnuts, add them after 20–25 minutes cooking.

make the beetroot straws: peel the beetroot and slice thinly, then cut the slices into matchstick size strips. Place on kitchen paper and leave to dry for 30 minutes. Pat dry well. Heat the oil to 180–190°C (350–375°F), or until a cube of bread browns in 30 seconds. Cook the beetroot strips in batches until crisp; drain on kitchen paper.

remove the pheasant from the casserole and keep warm. Skim off any excess fat from the juices. Place over a moderate to high heat and boil rapidly until the sauce reduces and thickens slightly. Check the seasoning, then serve with the pheasant, accompanied by the beetroot straws.

Serves 4
Preparation time: *30 minutes, plus
draining*
Cooking time: *1¼–1½ hours*

Quail *with peas and ham*

50 g/2 oz butter
1 tablespoon olive oil
4–8 quails, cleaned and trussed
125 g/4 oz gammon steak, finely diced
150 ml/¼ pint dry white wine
400 g/13 oz can tomatoes, drained, deseeded and chopped
375 g/12 oz shelled fresh or frozen peas
150 ml/¼ pint Chicken Stock (see page 10) if needed
salt and pepper
chopped flat leaf parsley, to garnish

heat half the butter and the oil in a flameproof casserole and brown the quails on all sides. Remove from the pan and add half the diced gammon. Cook until lightly coloured, then return the quail to the pan with the wine and tomatoes. Season to taste and bring to the boil. Cover tightly and cook in a preheated oven at 190°C/375°F/Gas Mark 5 for 20–25 minutes until the quails are just tender.

meanwhile heat the remaining butter in a pan and cook the remaining gammon until it is golden brown. Add the peas and, if necessary, a little water. Season lightly with salt and pepper. Simmer gently until the peas are tender and all the liquid has evaporated. Keep hot.

remove the cooked quails from the pan and remove any trussing strings. Place on a warmed serving dish and keep hot. Add the pea mixture to the pan and stir well over a gentle heat until the peas are coated with the sauce and are heated through. If necessary, add some chicken stock to the pan to give a coating consistency. Pile on the dish, garnish with chopped parsley and serve at once with creamed potatoes.

Serves 4
Preparation time: *20–30 minutes*
Cooking time: *40–50 minutes*
Oven temperature:
  190°C/375°F/Gas Mark 5

clipboard: If you are using fresh peas, choose young tender ones and add sufficient water to soften them but allow it almost to boil away by the time they are cooked. Frozen peas should need almost no water and will take only a few minutes to cook. Quails are very meaty little birds and you may find one is enough per person.

Braised Pigeon
with peas

4 tablespoons olive oil

125 g/4 oz lean bacon, diced

1 onion, chopped

1 carrot, chopped

1 celery stick, chopped

1 garlic clove, chopped

4 young pigeons, cleaned

7 tablespoons dry white wine

375 g/12 oz shelled fresh peas

pinch of ground cinnamon

450 ml/¾ pint Chicken Stock (see page 10)

salt and pepper

rosemary sprigs, to garnish

heat the oil in a flameproof casserole, add the bacon, onion, carrot, celery and garlic, and fry gently for 10 minutes. Add the pigeons and fry until browned on all sides, turning frequently. Add the wine and cook until it has evaporated.

add the peas, cinnamon, salt and pepper to taste, and the stock. Cover and simmer for 30 minutes or until the pigeons are tender, basting the pigeons with the cooking liquid occasionally. Serve hot, garnish with rosemary sprigs.

Serves 4
Preparation time: *15–20 minutes*
Cooking time: *about 50 minutes*

clipboard: Pigeons are most likely to be found in the freezer cabinet of the supermarket. Thaw completely before cooking and use a boning or cook's knife to cut them in half.

Pizza, Rice & Polenta

Basic Pizza Dough

The dried yeast used for this dough does not need pre-mixing with water, milk or sugar and can be added directly to the flour. It is sometimes called easy-blend dried yeast, so read the packet instructions carefully to ensure that you have the right one.

250 g/8 oz unbleached strong plain flour
I teaspoon fast-action dried yeast
I teaspoon salt
I tablespoon olive oil
125–150 ml/4 fl oz–¼ pint warm water

sift the flour, yeast and salt into a bowl. Make a well in the centre and add the oil. Gradually pour in the water, stir vigorously, drawing in the flour a little at a time, to form a soft dough. Knead for at least 10 minutes until the dough feels silky smooth and springy.

place the dough in an oiled bowl, turning once so the surface is coated. Cover the bowl with a cloth and leave to rise in a warm place for 1–2 hours until doubled in size.

when the dough has risen sufficiently, knock it back and turn it out on to a floured surface. Knead again for 2–3 minutes.

Makes enough for 1 x 30 cm/12 inch pizza,
2 x 20 cm/8 inch pizzas,
4 x 15 cm/6 inch pizzas or
6 x 12 cm/5 inch pizzas
Preparation time: *15 minutes, plus rising*
Cooking time: *see recipes*

Pizza Napoletana

Fresh yeast is used for this pizza dough, but you can use the Basic Pizza Dough made with fast-action dried yeast on page 158 if you prefer.

15 g/½ oz fresh yeast
2 tablespoons warm water
250 g/8 oz strong plain flour
1 teaspoon salt
2 tablespoons olive oil
3 tablespoons milk
1 tablespoon torn basil leaves, to garnish

Topping
4 tablespoons olive oil
400 g/13 oz can chopped tomatoes, drained
1 tablespoon chopped basil
1 teaspoon dried oregano
175 g/6 oz mozzarella cheese, sliced
4 tablespoons grated Parmesan cheese
salt and pepper

blend the yeast with the warm water in a small bowl. Leave in a warm place for 10 minutes until frothy. Sift the flour and salt into a large bowl, make a well in the centre and pour in the yeast mixture, oil and milk. Gradually draw the flour into the liquid and mix to form a stiff but pliable dough, adding more milk if necessary.

knead the dough on a lightly floured surface for about 5 minutes until it is light and elastic. Place in an oiled bowl, turning once so the surface is coated. Cover the bowl with a cloth and leave to rise in a warm place for 1 hour, or until doubled in size. Turn out on to a floured surface and divide into 2 or 4 pieces. Knead each piece lightly.

roll out the dough to cover two 23 cm/9 inch or four 15 cm/6 inch lightly oiled ovenproof plates. Alternatively, place a piece of dough on each plate and press it out, with floured knuckles, to cover the base.

brush with some of the oil, cover with the tomatoes and season. Sprinkle with the herbs, top with mozzarella, a sprinkling of Parmesan and a little more oil. Leave to rise in a warm place for 30 minutes. Bake in a preheated oven at 220°C/425°F/Gas Mark 7 for 15 minutes, then reduce the heat to 180°C/350°F/Gas Mark 4 for 5 minutes. Serve sprinkled with torn basil.

Serves 4
Preparation time: *15 minutes, plus rising*
Cooking time: *20 minutes*
Oven temperature: *220°C/425°F/Gas Mark 7*

Many Tomato Pizza

This pizza is topped with a variety of different tomatoes which make an interesting contrast in colours and flavours.

1 quantity Basic Pizza Dough (see page 158), risen
extra virgin olive oil, for oiling and drizzling

Topping

2 large ripe plum tomatoes, skinned and sliced
125 g/4 oz red cherry tomatoes, skinned and halved
125 g/4 oz yellow pear tomatoes, skinned and halved
4 sun-dried tomatoes in oil, drained and chopped
handful of basil leaves, torn into pieces
2 teaspoons grated lemon rind
12 black olives, pitted
sea salt and pepper

knead the risen dough on a lightly floured surface, divide in half and roll out each piece to a 23 cm/9 inch round. Transfer to 2 oiled pizza plates or a large oiled baking sheet.

dry the tomato slices on kitchen paper. Arrange all the tomatoes over the pizzas, scattering the basil, lemon rind and black olives on top. Season well and drizzle a little extra olive oil over.

place at the top of a preheated oven at 230°C/450°F/Gas Mark 8 for 20 minutes until the bases are crisp and the tops golden. Serve at once.

Serves 2
Preparation time: *10 minutes,*
  plus making the dough and rising
Cooking time: *20 minutes*
Oven temperature:
  230°C/450°F/Gas Mark 8

Spicy Hot Pizza

1 quantity Basic Pizza Dough (see page 158)
marjoram sprigs, to garnish (optional)

Topping

1–2 tablespoons olive oil
1 garlic clove, crushed
2–3 shallots, chopped
250 g/8 oz tomatoes, skinned, deseeded and
chopped
150 ml/¼ pint dry white wine
1 teaspoon dried mixed herbs
25 g/1 oz butter
2 red onions, sliced
2–3 green chillies, cored, deseeded and sliced
lengthways
1 tablespoon chopped thyme
1 tablespoon chopped marjoram
50 g/2 oz mozzarella cheese, diced
salt and pepper

first make the topping. Heat the oil in a pan, add the garlic and shallots and cook for about 5 minutes, until golden. Add the tomatoes, wine and dried mixed herbs. Bring to the boil and cook rapidly for 20 minutes, until thickened. Season with salt and pepper to taste and leave to cool.

melt the butter in a pan, add the onions and cook for 5 minutes until golden. Leave to cool.

knead the risen dough on a lightly floured surface, and roll out to two 23 cm/9 inch rounds. Transfer to a large heated, oiled baking sheet. Spread the onions on the pizza bases and cover with the tomato mixture. Sprinkle with the chillies, thyme, marjoram and mozzarella.

bake at once in a preheated hot oven at 220°C/425°F/Gas Mark 7 for 15–20 minutes, until the dough and topping are golden. Garnish with marjoram sprigs, if using, and serve immediately.

Serves 4
Preparation time: *20 minutes, plus making the dough, rising and cooling*
Cooking time: *40 minutes*
Oven temperature:
220°C/425°F/Gas Mark 7

Rosemary

Fennel

Basil

Chillies

Nutmeg

Dill

Marjoram

Sage

Chillies

The hottest spice of all. On the whole, the smallest chillies are the hottest ones. The seeds are always the most fiery part of all.

Nutmeg

Available whole, to be used grated, or ground, the nutmeg with its beautiful sweet flavour is the seed of a tropical evergreen tree. It is frequently found in Italian cooking particularly in bechamel and other sauces.

Rosemary

One of the herbs that shouts Italy very loudly (the others are basil and sage). Often used with lamb and chicken, rosemary is a very aromatic and strongly flavoured herb, so use with care. It dries very well.

Fennel

There are three types of fennel, two are grown primarily as a herb for their seeds and leaves and the third as a vegetable. Fennel has an aniseed flavour and goes well with fish.

Dill

A bright green feathery herb and very similar in appearance to fennel.

Marjoram

An aromatic herb with a sweet spicy flavour and very similar to oregano. Use with chicken, veal, pasta dishes and tomatoes. Marjoram is best added at the end of cooking.

Basil

Possibly the most important herb in Italian cooking, basil has soft bright green leaves and a superb flavour. Best known as the unique ingredient in pesto and for its affinity with tomatoes.

Sage

A herb with grey-green leaves and a slightly bitter flavour. The Italians often use it with veal and calves' liver dishes and to flavour cheeses. Sage can stand up to long, slow cooking.

Rich Polenta Salad

600 ml/1 pint water
150 g/5 oz instant polenta flour
25 g/1 oz butter
250 g/8 oz goats' cheese, rind removed, thinly sliced or crumbled
1 small radicchio head
125 g/4 oz rocket
3 tablespoons extra virgin olive oil
1 tablespoon balsamic vinegar
salt and pepper

heat the water to a gentle simmer, pour in the polenta flour and beat well for 1–2 minutes until it is a smooth paste. Turn the heat down and continue to cook the polenta until it thickens, stirring constantly, for 6–8 minutes.

add the butter and season with salt and pepper; mix well. Place the polenta on a chopping board and spread to 1.5 cm/¾ inch thick and allow to set for 5 minutes.

arrange the goats' cheese on the polenta, then cut the polenta into bars or wedges. Place the polenta under a preheated grill and cook until the cheese has melted and starts to bubble.

place the radicchio leaves and the rocket in a bowl. Add the oil and vinegar and season with salt and pepper, then toss the leaves until coated. Arrange the salad leaves on individual plates and place the polenta bars or wedges on top.

Serves 4
Preparation time: *10 minutes*
Cooking time: *15–20 minutes*

Baked Polenta

with Fontina

Fontina is a semifirm and creamy cheese from the Val d'Aosta in Northern Italy.

600 ml/1 pint water
150 g/5 oz instant polenta flour
125 g/4 oz butter, plus extra for greasing
handful of marjoram, chopped
200 g/7 oz Fontina cheese, grated
salt and pepper

Sauce

3 tablespoons olive oil
2 garlic cloves, crushed and chopped
1 onion, chopped
400 g/13 oz can chopped tomatoes
1 thyme sprig
1 teaspoon vinegar
1 teaspoon sugar
salt and pepper

heat the water to a gentle simmer, pour in the polenta flour and beat well for 1–2 minutes until it is a smooth paste. Turn the heat down and continue to cook the polenta until it thickens, stirring constantly, for 6–8 minutes.

add the butter and chopped marjoram and season with salt and pepper. Mix well. Place the polenta on a chopping board, roll out to 1.5 cm/¾ inch thick and allow to set for 5 minutes.

meanwhile make the sauce. Heat the olive oil in a saucepan, add the garlic and onion and sauté for 3 minutes. Add the tomatoes, thyme, vinegar and sugar. Season with salt and pepper and simmer for 10 minutes over a moderate to high heat until the tomatoes reduce to a thick sauce.

butter a shallow ovenproof dish, cut the polenta into squares and line the bottom of the dish with half of the squares. Sprinkle over half of the grated Fontina. Spoon over half of the sauce and top with the remaining polenta. Add the remaining sauce and the remaining grated Fontina and bake in a preheated oven at 200°C/400°F/Gas Mark 6 for 10–15 minutes until the cheese is golden and the sauce bubbling.

Serves 4
Preparation time: *10 minutes*
Cooking time: *30–40 minutes*
Oven temperature:
  200°C/400°F/Gas Mark 6

Spinach and Lemon Risotto

1 litre/1¾ pints Chicken Stock or
Vegetable Stock (see pages 10 and 11)
125 g/4 oz butter
1 tablespoon olive oil
2 shallots, finely chopped
300 g/10 oz arborio rice
500 g/1 lb spinach, chopped
grated rind and juice of 1 lemon
125 g/4 oz Parmesan cheese, grated
salt and pepper

heat the chicken or vegetable stock in a saucepan to a gentle simmer.

melt half the butter and the olive oil in another saucepan, add the shallots and sauté for 3 minutes.

add the rice and stir well to coat the grains thoroughly. Add a ladleful of stock, enough to cover the rice, and stir well. Simmer gently and continue to stir as frequently as possible, adding more stock as it is absorbed, reserving a ladleful.

stir in the chopped spinach, lemon rind and juice, reserving a little lemon rind for garnishing, and season with salt and pepper. Increase the heat, stir well then add the remaining stock and butter. Allow to cook for a few minutes, then add half of the Parmesan and mix in well. Serve sprinkled with the remaining Parmesan and lemon rind.

Serves 4
Preparation time: *5 minutes*
Cooking time: *about 30 minutes*

Milanese Risotto

150 g/5 oz unsalted butter
½ onion, finely chopped
400 g/13 oz arborio rice
7 tablespoons dry white wine
1 litre/1¾ pints chicken (see page 10) or vegetable
stock (see page 11), kept simmering
¼ teaspoon saffron threads
125 g/4 oz fresh Parmesan shavings
salt and pepper
basil leaves, to garnish

melt half of the butter in a large, heavy-based pan, add the onion, season with a little pepper and fry gently for about 5 minutes until softened.

add the rice and stir to coat thoroughly in the buttery mixture.

add the wine, a ladleful of the stock and the saffron threads, and cook over a low heat, stirring until all the liquid is absorbed.

continue adding the stock in this way, a ladleful at a time, and stirring until absorbed. The risotto is ready when all the stock has been absorbed and the grains of rice are tender and the risotto creamy and moist without being 'gluey'. (This will take about 20–25 minutes.)

remove the pan from the heat, stir in the remaining butter and the Parmesan shavings, garnish with basil and serve immediately.

Serves 4–6
Preparation time: 5–10 *minutes*
Cooking time: 25–30 *minutes*

Fish Risotto

50–75 g/2–3 oz unsalted butter

1 large onion, peeled and finely chopped

1.2–1.5 litres/2–2½ pints Fish Stock (see page 11)

1 celery stick, sliced

1 thyme sprig

2 parsley sprigs

1 mace blade

1 small onion, peeled but left whole and studded with 2 cloves

375–500 g/12 oz–1 lb arborio rice

150 ml/¼ pint dry white wine

500 g/1 lb monkfish, haddock, halibut or other firm white fish fillets, skinned and cubed

2 small red mullet, heads and tails removed, cut into 2.5 cm/1 inch slices (optional)

3–4 saffron threads (optional)

1 garlic clove, peeled and finely chopped

300 g/10 oz cooked unshelled prawns

40 g/1½ oz grated Parmesan cheese, plus extra to serve

sea salt and white pepper

finely chopped parsley, to garnish

heat 25 g/1 oz of the butter in a large pan, add the onion and cook for 5–10 minutes, until soft but not coloured.

meanwhile, pour the fish stock into another pan, then tie the celery, thyme, parsley, mace blade and studded onion in a piece of muslin and add to the pan. Bring just to boiling point, then keep at a gentle simmer.

add the rice (use the larger amount if omitting the mullet) to the onions, and stir until well coated. Pour in the wine, raise the heat a little and cook for 3–4 minutes until the wine has almost evaporated.

add a ladleful of the hot stock to the pan and cook on a low heat for 2–4 minutes, until the stock is almost absorbed, then add another ladleful. Stir into the rice. Continue adding stock, a little at a time, and stirring often, until you have added about 1 litre/1¾ pints. Add the monkfish and red mullet, if using, then a little stock and cook for 4–5 minutes.

place the saffron, if using, in a small bowl, pour over 3–4 tablespoons of the stock. Stir quickly to start the colour running, then set aside.

melt 15 g/½ oz of the butter in another small pan, add the garlic and prawns and cook for 3–4 minutes, then stir into the risotto. Add the saffron liquid, and another ladleful of stock if you have used the whole quantity of the rice. The rice should be tender and the risotto creamy and moist without being 'gluey'. Season with salt and pepper.

add the remaining butter and the Parmesan, stirring until melted, then heap into a warmed serving dish, sprinkle with parsley and serve at once with more Parmesan.

Serves 6–8
Preparation time: *20 minutes*
Cooking time: *45–55 minutes*

Stuffed Rice Croquettes

600 ml/I pint water
150 ml/¼ pint meat gravy
3 tomatoes, skinned, deseeded and chopped
50 g/2 oz butter
500 g/I lb arborio rice
6 tablespoons grated Parmesan cheese
3 eggs, lightly beaten
125 g/4 oz mozzarella cheese, diced
fine dry breadcrumbs, for coating
oil, for deep-frying
salt and pepper

Meat filling
50 g/2 oz butter
2 slices Parma ham, shredded
I small onion, finely chopped
125 g/4 oz chopped veal
2 tomatoes, skinned, deseeded and chopped
125 g/4 oz chicken livers, chopped
salt and pepper

bring the water to the boil in a large pan. Stir in the gravy, tomatoes and butter, and pour in the rice. Mix well and simmer over a low heat for 15 minutes, or until the rice is tender. Stir occasionally to prevent it sticking and add more water if necessary.

meanwhile, make the filling. Heat the butter in a saucepan over a moderate heat and sauté the ham and onion. Add the veal and cook until lightly browned. Add the tomatoes and simmer until reduced. Add the chicken livers and cook quickly. Season and remove the pan from the heat.

remove the rice mixture from the heat, and stir in the grated Parmesan and beaten eggs. Season with salt and pepper. Turn the rice mixture into a bowl and set aside to cool.

place a rounded tablespoon of rice in the palm of one hand. Make a depression in the centre and fill with some of the meat mixture and 2 cubes of mozzarella. Cover the filling with the rice and shape into a ball. Repeat with the rest of the mixture and coat the rice balls with breadcrumbs. Heat the oil to 180–190°C (350–375°F), or until a cube of bread browns in 30 seconds, and deep-fry the rice balls, a few at a time, until golden brown. Drain on kitchen paper and serve hot.

Serves 4–6
Preparation time: *20 minutes*
Cooking time: *45 minutes*

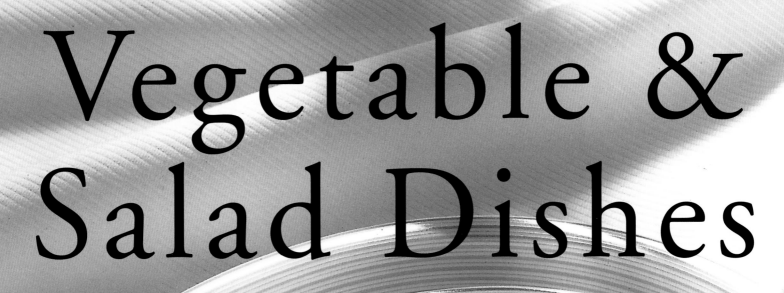

Vegetable &
Salad Dishes

Stuffed Courgettes

6 small courgettes, cut in half lengthways

2 tablespoons olive oil

1 large onion, finely chopped

200 g/7 oz arborio rice

25 g/1 oz butter

50–75 g/2–3 oz Parmesan cheese, grated

2 eggs

2 tablespoons milk

1 tablespoon chopped parsley

salt and pepper

cook the courgettes in a large pan of boiling salted water for 3–4 minutes. Drain well. Place under the cold tap until cool. Scoop out the seeds from each courgette half with a teaspoon and discard.

heat the oil in a pan and cook the onion until it is soft and golden brown. Meanwhile, cook the rice in a large pan of salted boiling water for 12–15 minutes until tender but firm to the bite; drain well and place in a bowl. Stir in the butter, half of the Parmesan and the onion. In another bowl, whisk together the eggs and milk and stir in the parsley and the remaining Parmesan. Season well with salt and pepper and stir into the rice mixture.

place the courgette halves in a well buttered ovenproof dish. Pile some of the rice mixture into each one and bake in a preheated oven at 200°C/400°F/Gas Mark 6 for 20–25 minutes until they are golden brown. Serve hot.

Serves 4
Preparation time: *25–30 minutes*
Cooking time: *35–40 minutes*
Oven temperature:
  200°C/400°F/Gas Mark 6

clipboard: This dish can be served as an accompaniment to a main course or it makes a good starter.

Fennel

Radicchio

Garlic

Red onion

Cherry tomatoes

Courgettes

Curly endive

Wild rocket

Cavolo nero

favourite, as a colouring for pasta as well as a vegetable.

Cherry tomatoes
The smallest and sweetest of tomatoes.

Curly endive
Also called frisé, this is a large, loose-headed lettuce-like member of the chicory family with a characteristic slightly bitter flavour.

Fennel
Its full name, Florence fennel, reveals its Italian origins. Italians eat it baked or braised with a sauce or raw, sliced with a dressing.

Courgettes
A favourite, cooked and eaten hot or cold. Courgette flowers are also delicious stuffed.

Radicchio
Part of the chicory family, this salad leaf has red leaves patterned with white.

Wild rocket
A peppery and aromatic salad herb, sometimes found under its Italian name *rucola* or the French name *roquette*.

Garlic
An essential flavouring in the Italian kitchen, where it is widely used.

Red onion
A mild member of the onion family.

Cavolo nero
A recent arrival in Britain, this very dark green, almost black, Italian cabbage is related to kale. It has a very strong flavour.

Aubergine Salad

This delectable salad can be served as a starter or as an accompaniment.

4 tablespoons olive oil

1 onion, chopped

2 garlic cloves, crushed and chopped

2 aubergines, cubed

4 tomatoes, skinned and roughly chopped

4 anchovy fillets, chopped

2 tablespoons pitted black olives

75 g/3 oz pine nuts, toasted

2 tablespoons chopped capers

handful of flat leaf parsley, chopped

salt and pepper

Italian Salad Dressing

1 tablespoon white wine vinegar

3 tablespoons olive oil

juice of ½ lemon

1 teaspoon Dijon mustard

salt and pepper

heat the olive oil in a saucepan, add the onion, garlic and aubergines and sauté for 15 minutes.

meanwhile make the Italian salad dressing. Place all the ingredients in a jar with a lid and shake well. Set aside.

add the tomatoes, anchovies, olives, pine nuts, capers and parsley to the aubergine mixture and season with salt and pepper. Pour in the salad dressing, mix well then allow the salad to cool before serving.

Serves 4
Preparation time: *10 minutes, plus cooling*
Cooking time: *15 minutes*

Peperonata

Peppers, tomatoes, onions and garlic braised in olive oil are the simple ingredients of this colourful Sicilian classic, although you could also add some chopped olives if you like. It is equally delicious served hot or cold.

100 ml/3½ fl oz olive oil
375 g/12 oz onions, finely sliced
2 garlic cloves, crushed
500 g/1 lb red and yellow peppers, cored, deseeded and quartered
500 g/1 lb ripe tomatoes or 400 g/13 oz can chopped tomatoes
salt and pepper

heat the oil in a heavy-based saucepan and gently fry the onions and garlic until they are lightly coloured.

add the peppers, cover and cook over a gentle heat for 10–12 minutes.

add the tomatoes and season generously with salt and pepper.

cook, uncovered, until the peppers are tender and the liquid has reduced to a thick sauce. Check the seasoning and pour into a serving dish.

Serves 4
Preparation time: *20 minutes*
Cooking time: *40–45 minutes*

clipboard: If you are using canned tomatoes, increase the heat toward the end of the cooking time so that the extra liquid evaporates. If you prefer, you can skin the peppers before you cook them.

Balsamic Braised Leeks and Peppers

Balsamic vinegar is regarded as the best and sweetest vinegar in the world. It comes from Modena where it is aged in wooden barrels for at least seven years and treated with all the reverence given to a leading château-bottled claret.

2 tablespoons olive oil
2 leeks, cut into 1 cm/½ inch pieces
1 orange pepper, cored, deseeded and cut into 1 cm/½ inch chunks
1 red pepper, cored, deseeded and cut into 1 cm/½ inch chunks
3 tablespoons balsamic vinegar
handful of flat leaf parsley, chopped
salt and pepper

heat the olive oil in a saucepan, add the leeks and orange and red peppers and stir well. Cover the pan and cook very gently for 10 minutes.

add the balsamic vinegar and cook for a further 10 minutes without a lid. The vegetables should be brown from the vinegar and all the liquid should have evaporated.

season well, and stir in the parsley just before serving.

Serves 4
Preparation time: *5 minutes*
Cooking time: *20 minutes*

Cavolo Nero with Pancetta

1 tablespoon olive oil
1 onion, sliced
1 garlic clove, crushed and chopped
1 red chilli, cored, deseeded and diced
125 g/4 oz pancetta, diced
1 head cavolo nero
75 ml/3 fl oz Chicken Stock (see page 10)
75 g/3 oz Parmesan cheese, coarsely grated
salt and pepper

heat the olive oil in a large saucepan, add the onion, garlic, chilli and pancetta and sauté for 5 minutes or until soft.

prepare the cavolo nero. Trim any wilting leaves then cut the head in half lengthways. Remove and discard the hard central stem and roughly chop the leaves.

add the cavolo nero to the onion mixture and stir well. Pour in the chicken stock and season with salt and pepper; cook for 4 minutes over a moderate heat, stirring all the time.

serve sprinkled with the grated Parmesan.

Serves 4
Preparation time: *5 minutes*
Cooking time: *10 minutes*

clipboard: Cavolo nero is a dark green Italian winter cabbage with long crinkly leaves. It becomes a brilliant green when cooked.

Mixed Grilled
Vegetables
with olive and walnut paste

Choose a selection of vegetables in season to serve with this rich green olive and walnut paste.

1 large aubergine, cut into 1 cm/½ inch slices
2 red peppers, cored, deseeded and halved, with
stalks left on
2 yellow peppers, cored, deseeded and halved, with
stalks left on
2 courgettes, sliced lengthways
8 baby leeks, trimmed and cleaned
6 tablespoons olive oil
4 large slices crusty country bread
salt and pepper

Olive and Walnut Paste
75 g/3 oz pitted green olives
50 g/2 oz walnut pieces
25g/1 oz bottled pickled walnuts, drained
2 garlic cloves, chopped
small handful of parsley
125 ml/4 fl oz extra virgin olive oil

first make the olive and walnut paste. Place the olives, fresh and pickled walnuts, garlic and parsley in a food processor or blender and chop finely. Gradually add the olive oil through the feeder tube until the mixture forms a stiff paste. Scrape into a bowl and season with salt and pepper.

spread the aubergine slices on a wire cooking rack over a tray and sprinkle with 1–2 teaspoons salt. Leave for at least 30 minutes to drain; this removes some of the liquid and bitter flavour. Rinse thoroughly, drain well and dry on kitchen paper.

brush the aubergines, red and yellow peppers, courgette and leeks with the olive oil. Place on the greased grill of a preheated barbecue or under a grill and cook the aubergines and peppers for 6–8 minutes, the courgettes and leeks for 3 minutes, turning frequently, until tender. Brush the bread with any remaining olive oil and grill until golden. Spread the toast with the olive oil and walnut paste and top with the vegetables.

Serves 4
Preparation time: *30 minutes, plus*
  draining
Cooking time: *10 minutes*

Roasted Courgettes

with Gruyère and tomatoes

6 courgettes
50 ml/2 fl oz olive oil
25 g/1 oz fresh breadcrumbs
4 tablespoons finely chopped basil
125 g/4 oz Gruyère cheese, cut into small cubes
250 g/8 oz cherry tomatoes, halved

cut the courgettes into 2.5 cm/1 inch thick rounds. Using a melon baller, scoop out the centre of each round but leave the bottom intact in each so the round is shaped like a cup.

heat the oil in a frying pan, add the breadcrumbs and cook, stirring, until golden and crunchy. Stir in the basil and set aside.

line a baking sheet with greaseproof paper and arrange the courgette rounds on it. Place a cube of Gruyère in each courgette round and top with half a tomato. Bake in a preheated oven at 180°C/350°F/Gas Mark 4 for 5–7 minutes or until the courgettes are just tender.

serve sprinkled with the breadcrumb and basil mixture.

Serves 10 as an appetizer or
  accompaniment
Preparation time: *25 minutes*
Cooking time: *about* 10 *minutes*
Oven temperature:
  180°C/350°F/Gas Mark 4

Potatoes Wrapped in Parma Ham

These delectable potatoes are equally good served as an accompaniment to a roast or nibbled as an appetizer with drinks. They are quite irresistable.

12 small new potatoes, cooked

12 very thin slices Parma ham

2 tablespoons olive oil

sea salt

roll each potato in a slice of Parma ham, patting with your hands to mould the ham to the shape of the potato.

oil a roasting tin, add the potatoes and cook in a preheated oven at 200°C/400°F/Gas Mark 6 for 20 minutes. Check the potatoes once or twice while they are cooking and turn them, or move them around, to ensure they cook evenly.

serve the potatoes sprinkled with sea salt.

Serves 4
Preparation time: *10 minutes*
Cooking time: *20 minutes*
Oven temperature:
200°C/400°F/Gas Mark 6

Tortino alla Toscana

Tortino is the Tuscan version of a thick, flat omelette, traditionally made with globe artichokes. It is similar to a frittata, but is usually baked in the oven; it is not turned over during cooking or grilled at the finish.

4 baby globe artichokes
6 tablespoons olive oil
I garlic clove, finely chopped
6 eggs
2 tablespoons finely chopped flat leaf parsley
salt and pepper

cut off and discard the tough ends of the artichoke stalks, if any. Pull off any coarse outer leaves, then cut across the tops of the leaves to neaten them. Cut the artichokes in half lengthways and remove any hairy chokes from the centres. Cut the artichokes lengthways again, into slices about 5 mm/¼ inch thick.

heat the oil in a 23 cm/9 inch frying pan with an ovenproof handle. Add the artichoke slices, garlic and salt and pepper to taste. Cook over a low heat, stirring frequently, for 10 minutes, or until the artichokes are tender.

beat the eggs and parsley in a jug, then pour into the pan. Bake in a preheated oven at 180°C/350°F/Gas Mark 4 for 20 minutes or until set. Serve hot, sprinkled with plenty of black pepper.

Serves 4
Preparation time: *10 minutes*
Cooking time: *30 minutes*
Oven temperature:
   180°C/350°F/Gas Mark 4

Finocchio alla Toscana

Anise-flavoured fennel is a great favourite in Italy. It makes a very good accompaniment to chicken and lamb.

625 g/1¼ lb fennel bulbs
1 thick lemon slice
1 tablespoon vegetable oil
25 g/1 oz butter
25 g/1 oz grated Parmesan cheese
salt and pepper
fennel fronds, to garnish (optional)

trim the fennel bulbs and remove any discoloured skin with a potato peeler. Cut vertically into 1.5 cm/¾ inch thick pieces. Place in a pan with a pinch of salt, the lemon and oil and add sufficient boiling water to cover. Cook for 20 minutes or until just tender. Drain well.

melt the butter in a gratin dish or shallow flameproof casserole, add the fennel and turn to coat. Season to taste with pepper and sprinkle with the grated Parmesan.

place under a preheated grill until lightly browned. Serve immediately, garnished with fennel fronds, if using.

Serves 4
Preparation time: *15 minutes*
Cooking time: *30 minutes*

Spinach with Egg

1 hard-boiled egg

500 g/1 lb spinach, shredded, or whole baby spinach leaves

25 g/1 oz butter

grated nutmeg

1 tablespoon lemon juice

1 tablespoon olive oil

salt and pepper

cut the egg in half and remove and reserve the yolk. Chop the white.

wash the spinach well and place in a saucepan with just the water that clings to the leaves. Cover the pan and cook for 7–10 minutes, shaking the pan occasionally, until the spinach is tender. Drain the spinach well and return it to the pan with the butter and a sprinkling of nutmeg, salt and pepper. Heat through, then remove from the heat and stir in the egg white, lemon juice and olive oil.

transfer the spinach mixture to a warmed serving dish and sieve the egg yolk over the top. Serve hot.

Serves 4
Preparation time: *15 minutes*
Cooking time: *10–12 minutes*

Asparagus, Bean and Pine Nut Salad

250 g/8 oz green beans
375 g/12 oz asparagus
3 slices wholemeal bread
3 tablespoons olive oil
1 Cos lettuce
50 g/2 oz pine nuts, toasted
50 g/2 oz Parmesan cheese, freshly grated

Dressing
2 tablespoons olive oil
2 tablespoons cider vinegar
1 egg yolk
1 garlic clove, crushed

cut the beans and asparagus into 5 cm/2 inch long pieces. Cook for 2 minutes in a large saucepan of boiling water. Drain and plunge into iced water. Drain again and wrap in a clean tea towel. Refrigerate until required.

remove crusts from the bread and cut into 1 cm/½ inch squares. Heat the oil in a frying pan, add the bread and fry until the cubes are golden brown all over. Drain on kitchen paper.

wash and dry the lettuce. Arrange on a large platter. Combine the beans, asparagus, croûtons, pine nuts and Parmesan. Place on top of the lettuce.

to make the dressing, combine all the the ingredients in a screw-top jar. Shake well and pour over the salad. Serve immediately.

Serves 4–6
Preparation time: *20 minutes*
Cooking time: *5 minutes*

clipboard: Pine nuts are best toasted by placing them in a slow oven for 8–10 minutes. Cover the salad with dressing just prior to serving.

Desserts &
Baking

Ice Cream Bombe

softened butter, for greasing
15–18 sponge fingers
about 175 ml/6 fl oz brandy
about 500 ml/17 fl oz hazelnut ice cream
about 500 ml/17 fl oz chocolate ice cream
sifted cocoa powder and icing sugar, to decorate

grease the bottom of a 1.2 litre/2 pint pudding basin lightly with the softened butter, then place a circle of greaseproof paper or non-stick baking parchment in the bottom.

check that the sponge fingers are not too long to fit inside the basin and trim off the ends if necessary. Pour the brandy into a flat dish.

place one of the sponge fingers in the brandy, turning it over several times until it is soaked. Work quickly, taking care that the biscuit does not break up. Stand the biscuit in the basin with the sugared side facing the basin. Repeat with the remaining biscuits to make a solid lining, working as quickly as possible. Fill in the bottom of the basin with broken pieces of biscuit, also soaked in brandy. Chill in the refrigerator for at least 30 minutes.

spoon the hazelnut ice cream into the centre of the basin, then spread it up and around the side to cover the sponge fingers completely. Freeze for about 2 hours until solid.

beat any remaining brandy into the chocolate ice cream, then use to fill the centre of the pudding. Level the top, cover with foil and freeze ready to serve.

remove the foil and carefully run a palette knife between the biscuits and the basin. Invert a chilled serving plate over the pudding, then invert them both. Carefully lift off the basin and remove the greaseproof paper circle. Decorate with cocoa powder and icing sugar and serve immediately.

Serves 8
Preparation time: *45 minutes, plus chilling and freezing*

Torta della Nonna

Pastry

175 g/6 oz plain flour
¼ teaspoon baking powder
pinch of salt
75 g/3 oz caster sugar
finely grated rind of 1 lemon
125 g/4 oz chilled butter, diced
1 egg yolk

Filling

2 eggs
2 egg yolks
50 g/2 oz caster sugar
4 teaspoons cornflour
finely grated rind of 1 lemon
300 ml/½ pint milk
300 ml/½ pint double cream
icing sugar, to decorate

first make the pastry. Sift the flour, baking powder and salt on to a cold surface and stir in the sugar and lemon rind. Make a well in the centre and add the butter and egg yolk. Rub in with the fingertips until the mixture resembles fine breadcrumbs. Gather the dough together, then roll it out gently to a rough round on a lightly floured surface. Lift the round into a 23 cm/9 inch fluted tart tin with a removable base and press the pastry into the corners and up the sides with your fingertips. Trim the top edge with a knife, then chill in the refrigerator for 30 minutes.

prick the bottom of the pastry case all over with a fork, then line with foil and fill with baking beans. Place on a heated baking sheet in a preheated oven at 190°C/375°F/Gas Mark 5, and bake blind for 15 minutes. Remove the foil and beans and set the pastry case aside, still on the baking sheet. Reduce the oven heat 160°C/325°F/Gas Mark 3.

to make the filling, place the eggs, egg yolks, sugar, cornflour and lemon rind in a bowl and whisk well to mix. Heat the milk and cream in a heavy-based saucepan until just below boiling point, then pour into the egg mixture, whisking all the time. Return to the pan and cook over a low heat until thickened, stirring constantly. Pour the custard into the pastry case and bake for 30 minutes or until the filling is just set.

leave the tart in the tin until lukewarm, then place on a serving platter. Serve warm or cold, with icing sugar sifted over the top.

Serves 6
Preparation time: *40 minutes, plus chilling*
Cooking time: *45 minutes*
Oven temperature: *190°C/375°F/Gas Mark 5*

Rags and Tatters

These carnival time fritters are popular in various regions of Italy where they are known by different names. The Tuscans call them cenci *because they are made from scraps, or bits and pieces, of dough.*

250 g/8 oz plain flour
1 teaspoon baking powder
¼ teaspoon salt
25 g/1 oz butter
4 tablespoons caster sugar
finely grated rind of 1 lemon
2 eggs, beaten
3 tablespoons sweet sherry
groundnut oil, for deep-frying
icing sugar, to decorate

sift the flour, baking powder and salt into a bowl, then rub in the butter with your fingertips. Stir in the caster sugar and lemon rind. Make a well in the centre and add the beaten eggs and sherry. Mix with a wooden spoon until a dough starts to form, then gather the dough together with your hands, adding a little more sherry if the dough is too dry.

turn the dough out on a lightly floured surface and knead until smooth. Leave to rest in a cool place for 30 minutes.

divide the dough into manageable pieces. Roll out the pieces one at a time on a lightly floured surface until very thin, then cut into strips measuring about 7 x 1.5 cm/3 x ¾ inches. Tie each strip into a knot.

heat the groundnut oil in a deep-fat fryer until 180–190°C/350–375°F, or until a cube of bread browns in 30 seconds. Drop a few fritters into the hot oil and deep-fry for 1–2 minutes until golden and crisp. Lift out with a slotted spoon and drain on kitchen paper while deep-frying the remainder. Sift with icing sugar while still warm.

Makes about 50
Preparation time: *20 minutes plus resting*
Cooking time: *19–20 minutes*

Cassata alla Siciliana

3 eggs, separated
125 g/4 oz caster sugar
finely grated rind of ½ lemon
3 tablespoons hot water
125 g/4 oz plain flour
1 teaspoon baking powder

Filling

175 g/6 oz caster sugar
3 tablespoons water
750 g/1½ lb ricotta cheese
500 g/1 lb mixed crystallized fruit
⅛ teaspoon ground cinnamon
75 g/3 oz plain chocolate, chopped into small pieces
8 tablespoons Maraschino liqueur

first make the sponge. Whisk the egg yolks with the sugar, lemon rind and hot water until light and foamy. Sift together the flour and baking powder and fold it gently into the egg yolk mixture.

whisk the egg whites until they are stiff, but not dry. Fold them into the sponge mixture. Pour the mixture into a buttered 25 cm/10 inch spring-form cake tin and bake in a preheated oven at 190°C/375°F/Gas Mark 5 for 15–20 minutes, or until the cake is golden and springs back when pressed. Turn the cake out and cool on a wire rack.

to make the filling, dissolve the sugar in the water over a low heat. Beat the syrup with the ricotta until well blended. Chop half of the crystallized fruit coarsely. Beat the cinnamon into the ricotta mixture, and put aside a few tablespoons for decoration. Stir the chopped fruit and chocolate into the rest of the mixture.

line the base of the cake tin with greaseproof paper. Cut the sponge in half horizontally and place one layer on the base, cut-side up. Sprinkle with half of the Maraschino, and spread with the ricotta mixture. Place the other sponge layer on top and sprinkle with the remaining Maraschino. Fit the ring of the tin in position and chill for several hours. To serve, remove from the tin, coat the top and sides with the reserved ricotta mixture and decorate with the remaining crystallized fruit.

Serves 6–8
Preparation time: *40 minutes, plus cooling and chilling*
Cooking time: *15–20 minutes*
Oven temperature: *190°C/375°F/Gas Mark 5*

Baked Stuffed Peaches

This recipe comes from Piedmont, in northern Italy, which is famed for its peaches.

4 large ripe peaches, halved and pitted
8 macaroons, crushed
4 blanched almonds, chopped
50 g/2 oz sugar
25 g/1 oz cocoa powder
7 tablespoons dry white wine
40 g/1½ oz butter
flaked almonds
icing sugar, to decorate

scoop a little flesh from the centre of each peach half, chop and place in a bowl. Add the crumbled macaroons, almonds, half of the sugar, the cocoa and 1 tablespoon of the wine. Fill the peach halves with the mixture and top each one with a small piece of butter.

arrange the peach halves in an ovenproof dish, pour the remaining wine over them, sprinkle with the remaining sugar and top with a few flaked almonds. Bake in a preheated oven at 180°C/350°F/Gas Mark 4 for 25–30 minutes, or until the peaches are tender. Serve hot, sprinkled with icing sugar.

Serves 4
Preparation time: *15 minutes*
Cooking time: *25-30 minutes*
Oven temperature: *180°C/350°F/Gas Mark 4*

Italian Cheeses

Fontina

Parmesan

Pecorino

Bel paese

Taleggio

Provolone

Fontina
A table cheese from the Val d'Aosta in northern Italy, Fontina is reminiscent of Swiss Gruyère, but softer and sweeter and with smaller holes. Made from cow's milk, it melts well and so can be used for cooking as well as eating.

Bel Paese
This mild soft cream cheese was first produced in Lombardy in the 1920s and is now made all over Europe.

Parmesan
A hard, grainy textured cheese used for grating. Only cheeses from the town of Parma in Emilia-Romagna are true Parmesan and bear the official stamp '*parmigiano-reggiano*' on their rinds. Buy in a block and store in the refrigerator.

Taleggio
A cow's milk cheese from northern Italy, which is similar in taste and texture to a mild Camembert.

Pecorino
This sheep's milk cheese is usually hard and sharp, as shown above, but it can also be soft and mild, as seen above right. When hard, it is similar to Parmesan and also used for grating and in cooking.

Provolone
A cow's milk cheese, originally from the south, which may be mild or piquant. Mature provolone is used in cooking, young provolone as a dessert cheese.

Mozzarella

Pecorino

Bocconcino

Gorgonzola and mascarpone tart

Ricotta

Dolcelatte

Mozzarella

A white curd cheese, originally made from buffalo's milk, with a soft chewy texture and a mild milky flavour. It is eaten fresh or used in cooking, particularly for pizza-making because of its excellent melting qualities.

Ricotta

A soft, very white fresh cheese made from the 're-cooked' whey of sheep's or cow's milk. Ricotta is used extensively in cooking, especially for desserts and baking. It is sold loose, cut from a round cake shape, or in plastic tubs.

Bocconcino

A fresh unripened cheese, shaped into small round balls, and sometimes referred to as baby or mini mozzarella. Bocconcino can be bought in plastic bags, packed in whey, with or without herbs. Store in the whey, in the refrigerator.

Dolcelatte

A soft, creamy blue-veined cheese (its name means sweet milk), dolcelatte is a mild mass-produced version of gorgonzola. Although it doesn't claim the classic status of that great cheese, it is extremely pleasant in its own right.

Gorgonzola and mascarpone tart

A comparatively recent development, this is a very rich dessert cheese made of alternate layers of gorgonzola and mascarpone. Because it is so rich, it is best eaten in small quantities.

Panettone Pudding

Panettone is a sweet yeast bread which Italians serve at Christmas. This recipe turns it into a version of bread and butter pudding.

50 g/2 oz butter
5 slices panettone
apricot jam, for spreading
250 ml/8 fl oz milk
250 ml/8 fl oz double cream
2 eggs
I egg yolk
50 g/2 oz brown sugar, plus extra for the crust

butter a 1.2 litre/2 pint ovenproof dish. Spread the panettone slices with the apricot jam and cut them into triangles or rectangles. Place in the buttered dish in overlapping layers.

pour the milk and cream into a saucepan and bring gently to the boil.

whisk together the eggs, egg yolk and sugar in a bowl until creamy and fluffy. Continue whisking and slowly add the hot milk and cream. When it is all combined, carefully pour it over the panettone, making sure that the custard mixture covers it. Sprinkle with a little extra sugar to make a nice crunchy crust.

fill a roasting tin with boiling water to make a water bath (*bain-marie*). Place the pudding in the *bain-marie* and bake in a preheated oven at 180°C/350°F/Gas Mark 4 for 25 minutes, or until the custard is set.

Serves 4
Preparation time: *15 minutes*
Cooking time: *30 minutes*
Oven temperature: *180°C/350°F/Gas Mark 4*

Lemon Polenta Syrup Cake

175 g/6 oz butter
175 g/6 oz caster sugar
125 g/4 oz ground almonds
50 g/2 oz flaked almonds
½ teaspoon vanilla extract
2 large eggs
finely grated rind and juice of 1 lemon
75 g/3 oz instant polenta flour
½ teaspoon baking powder
single cream, to serve

Syrup

grated rind and juice of 2 lemons
50 g/2 oz caster sugar
2 tablespoons water

line a 15 cm/6 inch cake tin with baking parchment.

beat together the butter and sugar until light and creamy. Add the ground and flaked almonds, vanilla extract and eggs and mix well.

add the lemon rind and juice, polenta flour and baking powder and mix well. Spoon into the prepared tin and bake in a preheated oven at 180°C/350°F/Gas Mark 4 for 25 minutes.

meanwhile make the syrup. Put the lemon rind and juice, caster sugar and water in a saucepan and heat through. Spoon over the cake as soon as it comes out of the oven. Allow the syrup to drizzle through. Serve the cake hot or cold with single cream.

Serves 4
Preparation time: *5 minutes*
Cooking time: *25 minutes*
Oven temperature: *180°C/350°F/Gas Mark 4*

clipboard: Polenta is made from cornmeal. Formerly a staple food for the peasants of northern Italy, it became fashionable in the late eighties. In the past it required about 45 minutes constant stirring, but instant polenta has reduced its preparation time to almost nothing.

Strawberry Water Ice

500 g/1 lb strawberries
4 tablespoons orange juice
150 g/5 oz caster sugar
4 tablespoons water
mint sprigs, to decorate

press the strawberries through a sieve, using a wooden spoon, reserving 4 whole ones for decoration. Stir in the orange juice.

gently heat the sugar and water, stirring, until the sugar has dissolved. Boil for 5 minutes, until syrupy. Cool, then stir into the strawberry pulp. Pour the strawberry mixture into a shallow container and freeze for 3–4 hours, until firm. Transfer the water ice to the refrigerator 30 minutes before serving.

slice the reserved strawberries in half lengthways. Serve the water ice in scoops decorated with the reserved strawberries and mint sprigs.

Serves 4
Preparation time: *10 minutes, plus freezing*
Cooking time: *5–10 minutes*

clipboard: When strawberries are out of season frozen ones can be substituted, although the flavour will not be as good. Choose a brand containing a minimum of sugar.

Mascarpone and Date Tart

This delightful dessert is a combination of soft cheese mixed with fruit.

150 g/5 oz plain flour
75 g/3 oz plus 2 tablespoons caster sugar
75 g/3 oz butter, chilled
3 egg yolks
250 g/8oz fresh dates, halved and pitted
250 g/8 oz mascarpone cheese
125 ml/4 fl oz double cream
2 eggs, lightly beaten
1 tablespoon cornflour
2 teaspoons vanilla essence

grease a 23 cm/9 inch fluted flan tin. Combine the flour, 75g/3 oz sugar, butter and egg yolks in a food processor and blend until the mixture just comes together. Turn the mixture out on to a lightly floured surface, and press together until smooth. Roll the dough, between two sheets of clingfilm, so that it is large enough to cover the tin base and sides. Ease into the tin and trim the edges. Chill for 20 minutes.

cut a sheet of greaseproof paper to cover the pastry-lined tin. Spread a layer of baking beans over the paper and bake in a preheated oven at 180°C/350°F/Gas Mark 4 for 10 minutes. Remove from the oven, and lift off the paper and baking beans. Return to the oven for 10 minutes until the tart is golden. Cool.

place the dates over the pastry base. Combine the mascarpone, cream, eggs, the 2 tablespoons sugar, cornflour and vanilla essence in a bowl and whisk until smooth. Pour the mixture into the pastry case and bake for 35 minutes or until the filling is golden and set.

Serves 8
Preparation time: *30 minutes, plus chilling*
Cooking time: *55 minutes*
Oven temperature: *180°C/350°F/Gas Mark 4*

Stiacciata Unta

This Florentine sweetbread is a modern version of an ancient recipe. Stiacciata *means 'squashed', referring to the fact that the bread is flat. It is eaten at carnival time in February.*

about 500 g/1 lb strong plain flour
½ teaspoon salt
1 sachet fast-action dried yeast
75 g/3 oz caster sugar
75 g/3 oz unsalted butter, at room temperature
2 egg yolks
200 ml/7 fl oz warm water
50 ml/2 fl oz orange juice
finely grated rind of 2 large oranges

To glaze
50 g/2 oz unsalted butter, softened
icing sugar

brush a 30 x 25 cm/12 x 10 inch roasting tin lightly with oil. Sift the flour and salt into a large warmed bowl, stir in the yeast and sugar, then rub in the butter with your fingertips. Stir in the egg yolks with a fork and make a well in the centre.

mix the water and orange juice with the orange rind. Gradually work the liquid into the flour mixture, then turn out on a lightly floured surface and knead for about 10 minutes until smooth and elastic. The dough is quite sticky, so work a little more flour into it as you knead, but take care not to add too much or the finished bread will be dry and tough.

turn the dough into the tin and stretch and pull it to fit the tin evenly. Wrap closely and leave to rise in a warm place for 1–1½ hours or until the dough is doubled in size. Unwrap.

bake in a preheated oven at 180°C/350°F/Gas Mark 4 for 30–35 minutes until golden brown. Remove the bread from the oven, brush with the softened butter and sift icing sugar liberally all over the top. Leave to cool in the tin for 20–30 minutes, then cut into rectangles and sift over more icing sugar if you like. Serve warm.

Makes 16 rectangles
Preparation time: *30 minutes, plus rising and cooling*
Cooking time: *30–35 minutes*
Oven temperature: *180°C/350°F/Gas Mark 4*

Garlic Focaccia

Panne all'pilo, *Italian olive oil bread has become universally popular. It is healthy and delicious, and not at all difficult to make — try this garlic-flavoured version.*

5 g/¼ oz dried yeast
1 teaspoon sugar
375 g/12 oz plain flour
175 ml/6 fl oz warm water
1 teaspoon salt
3 garlic cloves, crushed
2 tablespoons olive oil
1 tablespoon maize flour or semolina
1 tablespoon olive oil, plus extra for glazing
2 teaspoons finely crushed sea salt

combine the yeast, sugar, 1 teaspoon flour and the water in a small bowl. Stand, covered, in a warm place for 10 minutes or until foamy.

sift the remaining flour and salt into a large bowl. Add the garlic and stir with a knife to combine. Make a well in the centre, stir in the yeast mixture and olive oil. Using a flat-bladed knife, mix to a firm dough.

turn out the dough on to a lightly floured surface, and knead for 10 minutes. Shape into a ball, and place in a large, lightly oiled mixing bowl. Stand, covered, in a warm place for 40 minutes or until well risen.

sprinkle the base of an 18 x 28 cm/7 x 11 inch shallow baking tin with maize flour or semolina. Knead the dough for 2 minutes or until smooth. Press the dough into the tin, and prick deep holes in the dough with a skewer. Sprinkle lightly with water and place in a preheated oven at 200°C/400°F/Gas Mark 6. Bake for 10 minutes and sprinkle again with water. Bake for a further 10 minutes, brush with extra olive oil, sprinkle with the sea salt, then bake for 5 minutes. Serve warm or at room temperature, cut into squares.

Serves 4–6
Preparation time: *20 minutes, plus rising*
Cooking time: *25 minutes*
Oven temperature: *200°C/400°F/Gas Mark 6*

Olive Bread

1 tablespoon dried yeast
400 ml/14 fl oz warm water
750 g/1½ lb strong white flour
2 teaspoons salt
4 tablespoons olive oil
125–175 g/4–6 oz black olives, pitted and roughly chopped

sprinkle the dried yeast over the water in a small mixing bowl. Set aside in a warm place until foamy.

sift the flour and salt into a large mixing bowl and make a well in the centre. Pour in the yeast liquid with the olive oil. Mix well with your hand, drawing in the flour from the sides of the bowl, to form a dough.

place the dough on a lightly floured surface and knead well for 5–10 minutes, until the dough is elastic and smooth. Fold the dough inwards towards you with one hand while pushing it away with the other. Give it a quarter-turn and repeat. Put the dough in an oiled bowl, cover and leave in a warm place to rise until it has doubled in size.

knock down the dough to remove the air bubbles. Sprinkle with the olives and knead again. Divide the dough into 2 pieces and shape each one into a round loaf. Place on a greased baking sheet, cover with a cloth and leave in a warm place to rise again. Bake in a preheated oven at 230°C/450°F/Gas Mark 8 for 15 minutes and then lower the temperature to 200°C/400°F/Gas Mark 6 for a further 15 minutes. Cool on a wire rack and serve sliced.

Makes 2 loaves
Preparation time: *20 minutes, plus rising and cooling*
Cooking time: *30 minutes*
Oven temperature: *230°C/450°F/Gas Mark 8*

Index

Acknowledgments

Photo Credits
Sean Myers: front jacket, front flap, back flap
Graham Kirk: back jacket

Special photography by Graham Kirk

All other photos:
Octopus Publishing Group Ltd. / Bryce Attwell, Jean Cazals,
Gus Filgate, David Gill, Robert Golden, James Jackson,
Graham Kirk, Sandra Lane, William Lingwood, David Loftus,
James Merrell, Diana Miller, Hilary Moore, James Murphy,
Peter Myers, Sean Myers, Alan Newnham, Philip Webb,
Paul Williams

Front Jacket Home economist: Oona van den Berg
Home economist: Debbie Miller